AMERICA ANSWERS A SNEAK ATTACK: ALCAN AND AL QAEDA

Also by Gordon L. Weil

The European Convention on Human Rights

A Handbook on the European Economic Community
(editor)

A Foreign Policy for Europe

The Benelux Nations

Trade Policy in the 70s

The Gold War (with Ian D. Davidson)

The Long Shot: George McGovern Runs for President

The Consumer's Guide to Banks

Election '76

American Trade Policy: A New Round

Sears, Roebuck, U.S.A.

The Welfare Debate of 1978

AMERICA ANSWERS A SNEAK ATTACK: ALCAN AND AL QAEDA

GORDON L. WEIL

FIRST EDITION
1st Printing — September 2004

The Americas Group
9200 Sunset Blvd., Suite 404
Los Angeles, California 90069-3506
U.S.A.
Tel.   + (1) 310 278 8038
Fax   + (1) 310 271 3649
EM   hrmg@aol.com
www   AMERICASGROUP.COM

ISBN:
0-935047-52-2

Library of Congress Cataloging-in-Publication Data

Weil, Gordon Lee.
America answers a sneak attack : Alcan and Al Qaeda / Gordon L. Weil.-- 1st ed.
    p. cm.
Includes bibliographical references and index.
ISBN 0-935047-52-2
1. United States--Foreign relations--1933-1945. 2. United States--Foreign relations--2001- 3. Surprise (Military science)--United States--History. 4. National security--United States--History. 5. Alaska Highway--History--20th century. 6. African American soldiers--Alaska--History--20th century. 7. United States--Race relations--Political aspects--History--20th century. 8. Pearl Harbor (Hawaii), Attack on, 1941--Influence. 9. September 11 Terrorist Attacks, 2001--Influence. I. Title.

E806.W447 2005
940.53'2273--dc22

2004016230

FOR ESTHER GORDON

CONTENTS

Illustration

List of Tables

PREFACE AND
ACKNOWLEDGMENTS

December 7, 1941. September 11, 2001. These two dates stand apart from all others in American history. Early in the morning on each of these days, an organized, foreign force staged a sneak attack on the territory of the United States. The Japanese bombing of Pearl Harbor and the Al Qaeda terrorist attacks on New York and Washington laid bare the need for the adequate protection of the national territory — what has come to be known as homeland defense.

On the earlier occasion, words that President Franklin D. Roosevelt had spoken in his 1933 Inaugural Address once again were fitting, this time to a country reeling from the Pearl Harbor attack: "...the only thing we have to fear is fear itself...."

In December 1941, Roosevelt moved quickly to assure the American people that their government could defend the national territory against further attacks on either coast. What had been unthinkable a few days earlier became the highest national priority.

He soon decided that fear could be overcome by prompt and bold acts. At the same time as FDR approved a morale-boosting bombing raid on Tokyo, he ordered a road to be built to allow for the defense of unprotected Alaska, America's other major exposed Pacific territory. By this order he set in motion a project whose historic and symbolic values would far outstrip its military worth. The lessons taught by this road and its related projects — collectively, the Alcan — would be available to guide future leaders if the unthinkable ever happened again.

Alcan brought together significant strands of history. It embodied the rushed mobilization of the armed forces and civilian production in time of war without good intelligence to guide these actions. It was a station on the railway, no longer underground, to racial equality. It served as a testing ground for the international relations of a country now ready to accept its role as a world power. It was a cautionary tale of waste and arrogance. It helped make an unknown man into an American president.

Roosevelt assured Americans that defense of American territory would take care of itself in the future, as a result of the measures he was adopting. But September 11, 2001 showed otherwise. The Al Qaeda terrorist attack, a new form of war, provided a unique opportunity to apply the lessons from the immediate post-Pearl Harbor period. The results were disappointing: the failures of Alcan, recounted here, echoed down through the decades.

READER'S NOTES

Some guidance on use of terms in this book may be helpful. The Alcan Highway was a dirt and ice road built in northern Canada and inland Alaska in 1942. The road was improved to serve year-round with an all-weather surface, and the next year was renamed the Alaska Highway. A second, related project consisted of a series of airfields, begun even before the road and known as the Northwest Staging Route. The third related project was an oil pipeline system and refinery known as Canada Oil or Canol. Collectively, they are called Alcan or the Alcan projects. When referring only to the early road, it is called the Alcan Highway.

The book discusses the role of African American soldiers, but uses the applicable terms as they were applied by people in direct quotations: niggers, colored, negro, Negro, black. Some military units officially used the term "colored." The default term used is black. In Canada, people now called First Nations are called natives, as they were during the war. When quoting Canadian sources, the original spelling is used, e.g. defence and not defense. When citing dates, the military format of day-month-year is retained if that was used in the original document; otherwise month-day-year is used.

ACKNOWLEDGMENTS

Many people and institutions provided valuable help and advice in the development of this book. The appreciation recorded here cites a few of the most important contributors to this work. My thanks go to all who listened and helped.

Esther Gordon, my cousin, inspired me to write this book when she recounted the stories she had heard from her brother Col. Saul C. Gordon, a leader of the 97th Engineer Regiment, a regiment composed of African American enlisted personnel from Florida that helped build the road.

I interviewed some of the surviving African American veterans of the Alcan: Nehemiah Atkinson, Jesse Balthazar, Frank Brehon, Linton Freeman, Joseph Haskin, James Lancaster, Alexander Powell, and Irving Smith. In addition, Ed Carroll's son opened his files. These former soldiers recalled much and offered it all. I am deeply grateful.

Heath Twichell has written the authoritative history of the Alcan Highway. He was unfailingly helpful.

Helene Dobrowolsky of Whitehorse, Yukon, was the researcher for much of the book. She was creative, curious, hard-working and a source of sound advice. Her help was invaluable.

Among the institutions, several stand out. The Yukon Archives in Whitehorse are unbelievable: probably the largest collection on the Alaska Highway, well organized and easily available. While Americans like to complain about their government and its services, none could deny that the National Archives is the paragon of what one would like from a public agency. The staff is helpful, the collection is huge, and access is excellent. Two other libraries provided significant resources: the Rasmuson Library at the

University of Alaska, Fairbanks, and the Bowdoin College Library. The North Carolina Museum of History provided assistance on Southern maladies.

Godfrey Harris, publisher of The Americas Group, seized the opportunity to add this book to his list, for which I am most grateful. Nancy Provencal was immediately ready to put the book into shape for publishing, thus contributing to its timeliness.

Finally, I thank Roberta M. Weil, my wife, for her help, tolerance, advice and support on this project. We traveled the Alaska Highway together, just as we have traveled many other roads.

Gordon L. Weil

Harpswell, Maine
July 2004

America Answers a Sneak Attack:
Attack:
Alcan and Al Qaeda

PART I. AMERICA ANSWERS PEARL HARBOR

CHAPTER 1.

THE BIRTH OF HOMELAND DEFENSE

"Yesterday, December 7, 1941 — a date which will live in infamy — the United States of America was suddenly and deliberately attacked by naval and air forces of the Empire of Japan."[1] With these words, President Franklin D. Roosevelt reported to Congress on an event both infamous and rare, an actual attack on the territory of the United States. Hawaii was as much a part of the United States as the District of Columbia, where he spoke.

In the War of 1812, which it had started, the United States had learned, temporarily at least, that independence and the ocean separating it from Europe did not relieve it of the responsibility for defending the national territory. A Maryland lawyer, who witnessed the British naval bombardment of Fort McHenry at Baltimore in 1814, wrote in the forgotten fourth verse of a poem called "The Star-Spangled Banner": "Oh! thus be it ever, when freemen shall stand/Between their loved home and the war's desolation." In 1941, for the first time since then, Americans faced what Francis Scott Key had called "the foe's haughty host" on their own home territory.

Roosevelt went on in his Declaration of War Address: "The people of the United States have already formed their opinions and well understand the implications to the very life and safety of our nation." This war would not only be won, like the last global conflict, "to make the world safe for democracy," but would also be a war to keep America itself safe. "We will defend ... ourselves to the uttermost...," said Roosevelt.

Roosevelt had been talking with the American people in a series of radio broadcasts called "Fireside Chats" since he had taken office in 1933. On December 9, in the first of these talks after Pearl Harbor, he noted that "we have learned that our ocean-girt hemisphere is not immune from attack."[2] This observation was both a jab at the isolationists who had argued until the last minute that the United States could stay out of the war and a promise that defending the homeland was the first step on the path to victory.

The Pearl Harbor imperative for Roosevelt had three elements. The highest priority was to rally a stunned populace so it would be motivated, not demoralized. At the same time, the United States must begin rapidly to gear up the great productive potential of the American economy, first for defense and then for a massive, offensive war. Finally, Roosevelt must drive a spike through the heart of the isolationism that had grown since the end of the First World War, so that the United States could take its place as the world's first superpower.

On December 8, the President had spoken to Congress of the "righteous might" of the United States, a phrase embodying both the nobility of the cause and the ability to pursue it. Almost immediately, troops began to be deployed. Factories began to manufacture the weapons of war. But mere preparedness would not be enough in those early days.

On April 18, 1942, a raid on Japan by 16 aircraft under the command of Lt. Col. James H. Doolittle was meant to demonstrate to both the American and Japanese people that Pearl Harbor had undermined neither the morale of the American people nor their ability to respond early and forcefully to the military challenge. As a morale booster, its thrilling impact was enormous, leading eventually to a book and a hit movie called "Thirty Seconds over Tokyo." Coming four and one-half months after Pearl Harbor, it embarrassed the Japanese high command and caused profound and costly changes in its war strategy.[3]

Doolittle's raid took care of the morale issue. Americans were furious at having been caught by surprise. They were not demoralized. And they had learned the lesson that they could no longer be complacent about defending the national territory, that their land was no "fortress America."

But Doolittle's raid together with the Pearl Harbor attack brought home with perhaps unintended clarity that the vast Pacific Ocean was only a pond across which either the United States or Japan might be able to attack one another's territory. To be sure, the ability to launch such attacks depended on the ability to sneak across that great pond, and neither side could be sure just how able the other might be to stage a sustained attack or even an invasion.

Unlike the Doolittle raid, Pearl Harbor was no hit-and-run event. After destroying or damaging eight of the nine battleships of the U.S. Pacific Fleet, the Japanese quickly eliminated the smaller British Pacific fleet and overran Guam, Wake, Manila, Thailand and Hong Kong. Soon, some 500 million people would be under Japanese domination at a cost of only 15,000 of its troops.[4] A later congressional report would state: "This trend of events in the Pacific found Alaska, which lay on the Great Circle route, the shortest distance between the United States and Japan, in the most exposed position to attack."[5]

The Japanese had come in force and apparently to stay, at least for a while. While Admiral Chuichi Nagumo's fleet had quickly withdrawn to safety after its Pearl Harbor attack, numerous submarines remained in the waters between Hawaii and the West Coast. Three had accompanied the fleet itself and another five, each equipped with a mini-sub, joined in the attack. In addition, 20 other submarines, organized into three squadrons, were stationed near Hawaii and two more were sent on to the West Coast, soon to be joined by others. These subs comprised about one-half of the Imperial Japanese Navy submarine fleet.[6]

All of these submarines were long-range fleet vessels, large boats, seven of which could actually carry its own seaplane in a hangar on deck. They soon began to prey on the

West Coast. After Pearl Harbor, nine submarines were assigned to locations along major shipping routes on the coast.[7]

On December 20, 1941, off of Cape Mendocino, California, the unarmed tanker *Emidio* was shelled, torpedoed and sunk by a submarine in the First Squadron, previously assigned to Hawaiian waters. This attack established a pattern. In order to save torpedoes, a Japanese sub would surface and use its deck gun to shell an unarmed vessel and would use only a single torpedo, if necessary, to sink it.

Attacks off the California coast continued from December onward with at least nine more U.S. merchant vessels coming under fire or sunk in the next week, one off the mouth of the Columbia River.

The Japanese also shelled installations on land from their submarines. On December 30, 1941, a submarine lobbed shells into Hilo, Hawaii. Even more alarming were the shellings of an oil refinery at Ellwood, California, on February 23, 1942 and of Fort Stevens, Oregon, on June 21. And submarine reconnaissance brought Japanese seaplanes over Sydney and Melbourne, Australia, and Wellington and Auckland, New Zealand, and even over Pearl Harbor, again and again.

Although occurring much later but indicative of the perceived threat, as late as September 9, 1942, a seaplane from the Japanese submarine I-25 dropped incendiary bombs on a forest near Mount Emily, 10 miles northeast of Brookings, Oregon. The Japanese intended this attack as their response to Doolittle, although the Emperor's brother ordered that the pilot limit himself to trying to set off forest fires rather than bombing San Francisco or Los Angeles, as the naval aviator had suggested. Despite efforts by the U.S. Government to censor news of the attack, newspapers and radio stations awakened a worried public, which sought more defense for the West.[8] This first attack on the continental United States was followed on September 29 by another attack by the same plane on another Oregon forest. While this would be the last land attack from I-25, in the next two weeks, it would pick off four more vessels not far from the Pacific Northwest shore.

The Japanese seemed to have complete domination of the Pacific, right up to the shores of the United States. While it had taken a herculean effort for the Doolittle raid to drop less than 64 bombs on Japan, the I-25 by itself was able to drop four bombs, admittedly two of them duds, on the North American continent more than 10 months after Pearl Harbor and three months after the American naval victory at Midway, a feat the Americans could not duplicate.

The Japanese submarine fleet consisted of 64 boats, most of them new, located at key positions across the Pacific. By contrast, in addition to the three aircraft carriers that had avoided the Pearl Harbor attack and a battleship in drydock in Washington, the U.S. Pacific fleet consisted of 55 submarines, almost equally divided between Manila and Pearl Harbor. Even that was an illusion: 12 were almost useless antiques of the 1920s, some were undergoing overhauls and one was sunk on December 9. U.S. submarines had been used as scouts; before the outbreak of World War II, a Navy sub had never sunk a vessel.[9]

Alaska was vulnerable. The day after Pearl Harbor, Brig. Gen. Simon B. Buckner, head of the new Alaska Defense Command, wrote: "At dawn this morning I watched our entire Alaska Air Force take to the air so as not to be caught on the field. This force consisted of six obsolescent medium bombers and twelve obsolete pursuit planes."[10]

On December 23, 1941, Lt. Gen. J.L. DeWitt, head of the Western Defense Command, told the War Department by phone:

> He [Admiral Freeman, commandant of the Thirteenth Naval District] has only five destroyers – three he is using in Alaskan waters principally to protect our shipping going up with material and food for the command up there, and two in Puget Sound. That is so puny that he is almost helpless to assist me in what I've got to do up there.[11]

On January 3, 1942, Buckner reported to the War Department that "there is not at the present time a single up-to-date fighter plane" in his command and that there were only 23 planes for the huge area of the territory.[12]

A military problem, the defense of Alaska, began to become a morale problem. While there were numerous sightings of Japanese submarines, or at least their aftereffects, and the sub-based planes, the Army and Navy had no clear idea of how many enemy vessels they faced and whether their number was increasing or decreasing. Clearly, the Japanese could pin down the meager U.S. forces available in early 1942, simply by forcing the United States to defend the West Coast. By making the U.S. shoreline into the front line, the Japanese would have more time to consolidate their hold on newly occupied territories in the Pacific. In attacking Pearl Harbor, the Japanese had hoped to neutralize the Pacific fleet so they could gobble up Pacific real estate. They were aware of the U.S. war potential, but some in Japan hoped that the attack would demoralize the American people to the point that they would acquiesce in Japanese gains. Others reasoned that, by the time the United States was ready for war, Japan could have consolidated its hold on occupied areas.[13]

From the American perspective, clouded by inadequate intelligence, the situation appeared as bleak as the Japanese had hoped. On January 11, 1942 the carrier Saratoga was torpedoed. On January 23, the oiler *Neches* was torpedoed en route to Hawaii, forcing the cancellation of a projected American raid on Wake Island for lack of fuel.[14] In light of such success, would the Japanese attack long-ignored Alaska or at least neutralize it?

The situation was dangerous but not hopeless. With all of the uncertainty and fear about the Japanese, there was no belief that the Japanese could sustain an effective attack against the United States for any extended period. This reaction was based on something that required no intelligence, the fact that America's human and physical resources were great enough to overpower the Japanese, while also fighting a war in Europe.

And the answer for the defense of Alaska was self-evident. If you could not get there by water and if you had too few aircraft to get there by air, then build a road.

The idea of a road to Alaska was not new. With the increasing popularity of the motor vehicle, Americans took to the road and more roads were built. In the late 1920s, the premier of the Canadian province of British Columbia began lobbying for a road to Alaska through his province as a means of economic development. He received enough support in the United States, that, in 1930, President Herbert C. Hoover appointed a commission to study the idea. Because most of the road would have to be built in Canada, the commission not surprisingly estimated the cost to Canada at $12 million, far more than the cost to the United States of $2 million. Because the road was not then seen as having any military significance on either side of the border, the commission's support was essentially meaningless, since neither country would come up with the needed funds.[15]

In 1934, Alaska's congressional delegate Anthony Dimond, one of the great promoters of the road, introduced a bill to authorize the road and to study how to pay for it. His proposal called for appropriations of $100,000 for the study and $2 million for actual construction in Alaska.[16] In 1935, the U.S. House of Representatives' Committee on Roads recommended a highway.[17] Despite his support for the concept, Roosevelt opposed spending any money on it. The bill passed, without any appropriation, and Roosevelt assigned the follow-up work to the State Department. The matter progressed no further, because the Canadian federal government showed no interest in the proposal, which obviously would depend entirely on its willingness to cooperate and to invest a considerable sum, well beyond the ability of British Columbia by itself.[18]

Roosevelt was clearly interested in the idea and so were some members of Congress, especially those from the

Pacific Northwest. In 1936, the U.S. Minister to Canada raised the issue as did Roosevelt himself when he met with Canadian Prime Minister William Lyon Mackenzie King, whose dominance of the political life of his country paralleled Roosevelt's in the United States. The Canadian leader's notes reported the President as saying that the road "would be of great advantage for military purposes, in the event of trouble with Japan." If Roosevelt was accurately quoted, his remarks were extraordinary, because none of his military leaders had reached such a conclusion at that time. Mackenzie King responded that the road "was a matter which could be looked into but I could say nothing at present as to the possibility of any construction."[19]

After the outbreak of war between China and Japan in July 1937, Roosevelt's interest intensified as did his pressure on Ottawa. Less than three month's later, he visited Thomas D. "Duff" Pattullo, the new British Columbia provincial premier, once an opponent but now one of the most passionate advocates of the road, and their principal topic of conversation was the proposed highway.[20]

In 1938, Roosevelt appointed the Alaska International Highway Commission. This five-member commission was headed by Congressman (later Senator) Warren G. Magnuson of Washington, one of the leading boosters of the highway. Among its members was Ernest Gruening, Director of the Interior Department Division of Territories, responsible for the civilian governance of Alaska. Gruening would soon become Governor of Alaska, a non-elective, federal appointment.[21]

While it was obvious that this commission would support the highway and especially one routed through the State of Washington, Canada proceeded more slowly. Pattullo, whose province had jurisdiction over the roads that would be built there, had simply worn down MacKenzie King by a constant barrage of letters and public statements. The Prime Minister appointed his own commission, but named as chairman a man who was seriously ill and not expected to be available for service for six months.[22]

From here on, the push for a road to Alaska became bogged down in an alphabet soup of possible routes – A,B,C and D. Three of these routes had their advocates, American and Canadian, usually the politicians from places along the way that stood to profit from the construction and the tourists expected to follow.[23] Vilhjalmur Stefansson, a famed Arctic explorer, proposed Route D, which skimmed the northern edge of the Yukon and Alaska and had no immediate commercial value, although he claimed that it could open vast oil reserves. Once again, in 1940, the Committee on Roads issued a favorable report.[24]

Between 1930 and 1940, no progress had been made on the proposed road to Alaska. In part, this lack of action stemmed from a lack of funds on both sides of the border. During the discussions in this decade, both countries assumed that Canada would bear the cost of the road in its territory. Yet Canada was worried about U.S. domination and unsure about its role in a future war with Japan. It was not a willing partner, which would be essential to the construction of the road.

Few yet cared much about Alaska. Except for a few Gold Rush years at the turn of the Twentieth Century, the territory remained "Seward's Folly," so named for Lincoln's Secretary of State who had negotiated its purchase from the Russians. Alaska's population in 1940 was less than 73,000, including 500 military, only 9,000 more than its 1900 population. Nevada, the smallest state, had a population of 110,000 and the territory of Hawaii, with huge military and naval installations and an inviting climate, had 423,000. To sense how many Americans thought of Alaska, consider the attitude of ignorance and indifference of most Americans now to the remote territory of American Samoa. At a time of severely limited resources, the lack of interest in building a road to Alaska was understandable.

Roosevelt's ability to press forward was also hindered by a clear lack of enthusiasm among the U.S. military. On August 2, 1940, Secretary of War Henry L. Stimson had written to the House Committee on Roads that "the value of the proposed highway as a defense measure is negligible."[25]

But the prelude to war was causing changes in thinking about a road even before Pearl Harbor. In fact, a series of actions by the Japanese and Germans served to move the proposed highway up the list of military priorities from its previous oblivion.

Relations between the United States and Japan were deteriorating rapidly. In 1939, a treaty of commerce and navigation, the normal and basic economic relationship agreement between nations, was terminated. In June 1940, Japan successfully demanded that Britain shut down its Burma Road supply route to China. At that point, the Army established the Alaska Defense Command, obviously reflecting a newfound concern about the territory's possible vulnerability. Yet the new command was inadequately supplied.

Despite recognition of the possible vulnerability of the North American continent to Japanese military action, the need for a highway remained unproven in the eyes of the military. Both the United States and Canada believed that "so long as the fleet of the U.S.A. remains in being she [Japan] is unlikely to attempt any large scale operations against the North American continent."[26] General Buckner, the commander in Alaska, agreed that a threat from Japan would not arise if the U.S. fleet continued to dominate the Pacific.[27] Prophetic words.

But there was at least some slight interest at the highest levels of the War Department. In early 1941, General George C. Marshall, the Army Chief of Staff, listened to Stefansson's views, presumably because the explorer had no private, commercial interest in the proposed highway. Stefansson was an Arctic romantic, who saw the frozen North through the eyes of an outdoorsman impervious to the cold, not from the perspective of military practicality, and his advice was of little value. But Stefansson kept plugging away, publishing articles in *Harpers* and *Foreign Affairs* in support of the road. So far as the Army could see, the highway was mainly the project of dreamers or those seeking commercial gain.

When, on February 5, 1941, Delegate Dimond again introduced a bill to authorize a highway, it once again went nowhere. Few were paying attention to the fact that the demands of Lend Lease shipping and the neutrality patrol would require the transfer of a portion of the Pacific Fleet to the Atlantic, leaving Hawaii and Alaska more vulnerable.

Operation Barbarossa, the German invasion of the Soviet Union on June 22, 1941, changed perspectives. Despite a non-aggression treaty between Japan and the Soviet Union, signed just two months earlier, no one, including the Soviets, could be sure that Japan would not attack Siberia in support of its Axis partners. The Soviets asked immediately for U.S. support in case Japan attacked. That would bring the war to Alaska's doorstep.

On June 22, the Army began planning for long-range air patrols and issued an alert for Alaskan defense. The next day, in a remarkable about face from the Army's previous indifference to the road, Lt. Gen. Stanley D. Embick, responsible for U.S. military relations with the Canadians, wrote General Marshall that "the progress of events had inclined me to the view that the construction of an Alaska road is advisable as a long range military measure, provided its construction is controlled so as not to delay other more pressing military construction requirements, such as aviation fields."[28] While this was hardly a ringing endorsement, it represented a change of policy, which Marshall approved.

The Japanese themselves had paid attention to the possibility of an Alaska military road. The U.S. reported to Canada that an article in *Hoichi*, the official newspaper of the Japanese Imperial Army, had cautioned that the construction of such a road "will be regarded as a continuation of the horseshoe-shaped encirclement of Japan by the Washington Government."[29]

Although they were inching closer to an agreement that the Alaska road would make a good idea militarily, the Canadians remained unconvinced that they should devote increasingly scarce wartime resources toward building the road, while the Americans were lulled into a sense of security by the ships anchored at Pearl Harbor.

The Army finally stopped opposing the Dimond bill. By October 6, 1941, Stimson reversed himself in a letter to the Roads Committee, echoing Embicks's message and saying that "from an evaluation of the trend in international affairs, the construction of this highway now appears desirable as a long-range defense measure."[30] Still, no action was taken to pass the bill, because the Army continued to assign it a "low priority."[31]

On the eve of Pearl Harbor, the supposedly all-powerful Roosevelt had been unable to convince the Army that a road was needed, while Congress waited for a push from the War Department to do more than talk about the road, and the Canadians waited and worried. The stage was set for an effort to defend Alaska, and the need was no longer disputed. But wishful thinking caused the American government to dither about taking action.

The Japanese provided the needed clarity. Their attack suddenly not only exposed the vulnerability of the West Coast and Alaska, but made it a reality. Now, defending the homeland would become a high priority with no cost too great.

Army strategy called for the use of air power as the primary method of defending Alaska. It ordered 13 B-26 bombers and 25 P-40 fighters to Alaska, via Canada, in December. Only eight bombers and 13 fighters made it to Alaska. A stunning 11 of the planes had crashed on the way, and the other planes that failed to get through simply could not cope with the winter operating conditions.[32] Obviously, this was a disastrous start to the attempt to defend Alaska.

Roosevelt, who presumably needed little convincing, received a memo on January 14, 1942 reporting that the military forces in Alaska were "considered seriously inadequate to deal with even minor threats by our clever and determined enemy."[33]

The push that made the difference came from Ruth Hampton, Acting Director of the U.S. Department of the Interior, which administered the Alaska Territory. By that time Gruening, who had been responsible for territorial administration in Interior, had become Alaska's Governor.

On January 14, Hampton wrote Secretary of the Interior Harold Ickes, one of the President's close political advisors, that "a matter affecting national defense which occurs to me to be worthy of Cabinet consideration is the construction of the so-called international highway.... [T]he war in the Pacific...places such a heavy responsibility upon ocean-borne commerce...a land connection between the States and Alaska takes on an entirely new and possibly critical importance."[34]

Finally, the road received priority attention. On January 16, Ickes raised the matter at a Cabinet meeting, where, for the first time, both the civilian and military implications were considered. Of course, the civilian aspect had passed from economic development to simple survival. Supply for both military and civilian purposes would be threatened if the Japanese were able to continue or even increase their submarine attacks on West Coast shipping.

The Cabinet discussion was short. Roosevelt, after hearing from Ickes, ordered the establishment of a special Cabinet committee, composed of the Secretaries of War, Navy and the Interior. The committee was told to report back to the President with its recommendations "on the necessity for a road and the proper route." Planning for the highway to defend Alaska began almost simultaneously with planning for the Doolittle raid.

The initiative passed immediately to the War Department, whose support was essential. Interior's civilian needs could not trigger the required allocations of resources. In exchanges with the President during January, Admiral King, the Chief of Naval Operations, argued that a highway was not necessary because the Navy could protect coastal shipping, but he would not "categorically commit the Navy to insuring uninterrupted sea communications to Alaska under all circumstances," a position which the Army considered "equivocal and unsatisfactory."[35] In the absence of an iron-clad guaranty, however incredible it would be for any armed forces entity to give such an assurance in time of war, the Navy was pushed aside.

Within the War Department, the battle was joined. The Transportation Branch opposed "diverting funds, materials, engineering talent and labor [needed] for more pressing National Defense undertakings."[36] This position would actually mean that the Army, now faced with real war, would have to back away from its tepid support of the road. The War Plans Division initially saw building the road during wartime as a way to get Canada to go along with the project, but the Division also saw many practical drawbacks. It would be cheaper, less labor-intensive and possibly faster to build more ships. In fact, the road might not be ready in time to be of any defensive use, it said. And the Division assumed that Congress would still need to be convinced to authorize funds. Yet, without great enthusiasm, it reported that security of supply lines more than offset these obvious drawbacks.[37]

The Cabinet committee received this report on February 2, 1942, and it immediately became the Army's recommendation. Route selection, hotly contested over the years and still unresolved, would be left to the Corps of Engineers. The committee asked for an engineering construction plan. Brig. Gen. C.L. Sturdevant, the assistant chief of the Corps of Engineers, provided the report just two days later.[38] The road was on its way.

There was just one more formality. On February 4, General Marshall asked Admiral King for "a brief statement as to the ability of the Navy, considering all its commitments and probable future requirements, to maintain, under all circumstances, uninterrupted communications"[39] with Alaska. King replied that guarantees were impossible, but denied that Japan could seize any territory in Alaska that would allow it to prevent the delivery of supplies by sea, thus making the road necessary. Whatever King thought was certain to be ignored; the Army had decided.

Concern about the Pacific Fleet itself may have been present in the mind of Roosevelt, who regarded himself as a Navy man on the strength of his previous service as Assistant Secretary of the Navy, as well as being of concern to the Cabinet members. The Fleet had been caught sleeping at Pearl Harbor, and its losses were enormous. Could leaders have confidence in its promises? Either to save it from embarrassment in case its assurances could not be sustained or to give it some breathing space, it may have seemed wise not to depend too heavily on it. And the Battle of Midway, where it would regain the initiative in the Pacific, was still five months away.

Roosevelt was obviously satisfied with the decision to build the road, which he had long favored. In 1941, as the possibility of war loomed larger, Congress had appropriated $100 million for use at his discretion. For Congress to give the President such a blank check appropriation was extremely rare. On February 11, the President committed the United States to building the road, leaving the details to the Corps of Engineers and the Public Roads Administration. He also decided to draw $10 million from his discretionary fund to get the road started without delay, the first withdrawal since the fund had been authorized. The President understood that the military need would only be met by prompt action and that the public, especially in the West, needed reassurance that they would be defended. Roosevelt may have remembered the major, albeit peacetime, mobilization under his distant relative Theodore Roosevelt that had created the greatest engineering achievement in the Western Hemisphere, the Panama Canal. Now, at war only four decades later, the United States could create a new engineering marvel of similar magnitude, that would both answer the challenge to mobilizing both military and civilian forces and leave a monument to rival Cousin Teddy's.

How real was the Japanese threat? John Dower, the official British historian, said that the Japanese victories led to the belief "in the invincibility of Japanese air power, a belief which was given strength by the ease with which the enemy outmatched the obsolescent Allied aircraft. It created the myth of Japanese superiority... which took a long time to die."[40]

Could the Japanese actually mount a sustained attack on the United States? The so-called "Yamaguchi plan," of which the Americans were aware, called for the occupation of the Aleutians and Hawaii in order to force Roosevelt to negotiate with them.[41] The United States also knew later in 1942 of a message to the Japanese invaders of Alaska's Aleutian islands: "The important task is to secure to the fullest extent the present important area where our northern garrison unit is situated in the Western Aleutians, to break up the enemy's united attack, check the bond between the United States and Russia and to make preparations for future assault operations."[42]

A wartime propaganda film revealed Washington's thinking: "From Alaska, the Aleutian Islands stretch out like stepping stones to Japan. If Japan could scramble over those stepping stones from the east and gain a foothold on the mainland of Alaska, she might be able to cripple our shipping in the North Pacific and launch an aerial or amphibious attack against our West Coast."[43] In fact, Attu, the last of the Aleutians, was about 1,400 miles from Japanese territory. Going that same distance to the east, you would still be in the Aleutian chain, not yet to Anchorage.

The decision to build the road to Alaska, so long denied, came only after the Japanese had seemingly forced it on the United States. Even then, the Army had mixed feelings, and the Navy remained opposed. Congress would not act without a push from the Army. The President would not act without support from his military leaders. Why did they act, given their doubts about the road's value?

"Looking back at the Japanese attack on Pearl Harbor after fifty years it is hard to imagine the fear and alarm that gripped people," wrote one analyst in 1992.[44] Looking back from a vantage point after September 11, 2001, it is less

difficult to imagine that fear and alarm. Understanding public sentiment makes it easier to understand how a decision,
destined to involve tens of thousands of soldiers and civilians, and to cost the equivalent of billions of dollars could
have been made in the light of competing needs and limited
resources. As much as leaders might want to avoid use of
the word, the decision to build the road demonstrates that
one should not underestimate the power of panic.

Reason flees before panic. If the threat was strategically
accurate, would not building a road make a Japanese invasion even easier? The loss of Alaska to the Japanese was
clearly not impossible and would require the assignment of
a huge military force to drive them out. In the wake of the
surprise Japanese attack, caution suggested planning for the
absolute worst case. No record indicates that military leaders harbored genuine fears of such an imminent threat, but,
after Pearl Harbor and the cashiering of the officers in
charge there, certainly none would want to be responsible
for a lack of preparedness.

Neither as dramatic nor as risky as Doolittle's raid, the
Alcan Highway would nonetheless be the first large-scale
undertaking and the first major deployment of ground
forces of the United States in the war. Only one detail
remained: to get the Canadians to agree.

CHAPTER 2.

THE RELUCTANT ALLY

The American relationship with Canada is more complex than Americans generally understand. That lack of understanding, unchanged over time, clouded the judgement of the Alcan advocates and of the U.S. military, even as American attitudes toward the need for the road changed.

Americans often regard Canadians as being "just like us." They are not, and the root of the differences lies in history. The United States was formed in rebellion around a series of principles, an ideology, embodied in its fundamental documents, the Declaration of Independence and the Constitution. Canada, a colony that became a dominion that became an independent country after a gradual evolution, lacks the American ideological basis. Instead, its defining characteristic is its strong identity, perhaps defined by what it is not – British, French or American.[45]

The findings of a sociological survey of Anglophone Canadians during the 1930s revealed something of how Canadians thought of themselves and of Americans:

> The typical American, in Canadian eyes at least, was brash and arrogant, with little respect for law and order....

> It is noteworthy that the qualities which seemed to distinguish Canadians — and to reveal their superiority — were qualities which clearly reflected conservative attitudes. The emphasis was on respect for traditional institutions.... Rugged individualism was not necessarily seen as a sin but it was closely tempered by values associated with...social conformity....[46]

Overlaying this basic cultural difference were three elements of geopolitical reality influencing Canadian leaders, especially Mackenzie King, as the world moved toward war. First, Canada benefitted from the hemispheric security provided by its powerful neighbor. Prime Minister Sir Wilfred Laurier admitted in 1902 that the Monroe Doctrine, originally a statement of policy by a southward looking American president, protected Canada against aggression.[47] Laurier implicitly acknowledged that Canada expected no aggression by the United States itself.

Somewhat in conflict was the second reality: Canada's fear of American domination. The two countries lived together alone on the same continent, but the Canadians were outnumbered by more than 11-to-1.[48] Americans and their culture continually came over the border and with them also came the attitude that the Canadians really had no choice but to go along with what Uncle Sam wanted. Part of any prime minister's kit in Canada was (and is) a healthy skepticism about American intentions that could undermine Canadian sovereignty.

The third reality was the product of Canada's gradual evolution away from Britain. It wanted at the same time to be taken into the closest councils of both Britain and the United States, but not to be taken for granted by either of them. To assert its growing sense of its own sovereignty, Canada would have to use the United States to keep Britain somewhat at bay,[49] while not neglecting its historic obligations to a country whose King still was the Canadian chief of state. British Prime Minister Churchill had said that Canada was "a magnet exercising a double attraction, drawing both Great Britain and the United States toward herself and thus drawing them closer to each other."[50] Not surprisingly, French-speaking Canadians were especially pleased to have an American alternative to Britain.

From the first time the Alaska road was suggested, Mackenzie King felt all three of these pressures. The initial efforts to promote the road were commercial and American. In the early 1930s, a group of Seattle businessman proposed to finance the road privately in return for gasoline station and hotel concessions. Canadians regarded the proposal as a threat to their economic sovereignty, and it turned many of them against the road. The 1933 report of the commission appointed by President Hoover, calling for $12 million in Canadian spending for the road, hit the same note.[51]

While these early efforts could be safely disregarded, Mackenzie King had a more difficult time with the persistent premier, T.D. "Duff" Pattullo of British Columbia. Because Roosevelt had met with Pattullo and because of the province's jurisdiction over its own roads, Mackenzie King could not ignore him. But the Prime Minister did not like his provincial premier dealing directly with the President of the United States. Pattullo absolutely infuriated him when he proposed to borrow $15 million from the United States in order to build the road. "Grounds of public policy would not permit the funds of a foreign Government to construct public works in Canada," he concluded. "It would be ... a matter of financial invasion or... financial penetration."[52] Actually, his concerns went much further. Mackenzie King worried that the U.S. could simply seize the right-of-way in time of crisis, just as it had appropriated the Panama Canal.[53] The Prime Minister was also undoubtedly aware of how fragile the hold of the Canadian federal government was on its northern territories and thus loath to see a massive American presence there.

A royal commission was then studying federal-provincial relations, and Pattullo's direct contacts with Washington could only complicate matters. Finally, the Depression had strangled government revenues in Canada, and Mackenzie King did not want to ship funds from central Canada to B.C. to build a road in one of the most sparsely populated areas of the country.[54] Under a barrage of Pattullo speeches and letters, Mackenzie King would not go any further than his desultory support of a Canadian study commission.

The Canadians also had a growing concern that the United States wanted the road for military purposes. In 1938, Ruth Hampton, at the Interior Department, wrote a memo saying: "News releases from Canada indicate that military involvement is one of the chief fears which retards negotiations for the highway.... Never so far as I know has the military feature of this highway been proposed as one of its major justifications."[55] Or minor, she might have written, given the extreme indifference to the proposal at that time in both the War and Navy Departments.

The absence of any reference to the possible military use of the road only stirred up more concern. Writing in the Vancouver, B.C., *Sun* in 1939, reporter Bruce Hutchinson defined Canadian fears as "this latest fear — the vague feeling that Canada must...keep free of the military policies of the United States and of all other nations." He concluded: "An American financed highway could be nothing less than a military highway, which, by tying us to American foreign policy would, forever, prevent our being masters in our own house."[56] This fear was perhaps based on worries about a continuing U.S. military presence in Canada, but, more broadly, it contained the seeds of truth.

The Canadians seemed to pay little attention to the first Roosevelt statement on mutual defense, made in Chautauqua, New York, on August 14, 1936. "Our closest neighbors are good neighbors," he said. "If there are remoter nations that wish not good but ill, they know that we are strong; they know that we can and will defend ourselves and defend our neighborhood."[57] In a still fiercely neutral United States, here was the American president pledging to "defend our neighborhood." The Monroe Doctrine was still alive and well.

Two years later, on August 18, 1938, Roosevelt went even further in a speech delivered in Kingston, Ontario, saying: "The Dominion of Canada is part of the sisterhood of the British Empire. I give to you assurance that the people of the United States will not stand idly by if domination of Canadian soil is threatened by any other empire."[58]

These words had been inserted in the State Department draft in Roosevelt's own handwriting.[59] In the developing relationship with Canada, the American leader was unique.

Neither before nor since has an American president had such a good knowledge of Canada. Not only was New York, of which he had been a lifelong resident and governor, a border state, but he had spent almost every summer on Campobello Island in the Canadian province of New Brunswick. The President was more mindful of Canadian sensitivities and its importance to the United States than most of his fellow Americans.

This time, the Canadian Prime Minister picked up the cue. "We, too, have our obligations as a good friendly neighbor," he said two days later, "and one of these is to see that, at our own instance, our country is made as immune from attack or possible invasion as we can reasonably be expected to make it, and that, should the occasion ever arise, enemy forces should not be able to pursue their way either by land, sea or air, to the United States across Canadian territory."[60] While this statement may now seem self-evident, it marked a new stage in Canadian-American relations. But it was more an oratory flourish than a useful pledge, because the entire Canadian armed forces consisted of 9,400 personnel at the outbreak of war in Europe in September 1939.[61]

The fall of France in 1940 had created a new strategic situation that forced the United States, Britain and Canada to reconsider their military relationships. Contrary to Churchill's magnet analogy, it was Britain, not Canada, which drew the parties together, because Britain was in mortal danger. Roosevelt had made clear to Churchill that he would do all he could to support Britain, but he was faced in November 1940 with a presidential election for an unprecedented third term. His success depended in part in not directly confronting American public opinion, still heavily influenced by the isolationists.

So here were the players as the war in Europe heated up. Britain, virtually alone against Germany, needed the support of the United States, "the arsenal of democracy." To provide for its own defense, Canada needed to draw closer to the United States and also do what it could to help Britain.[62] Roosevelt needed, or at least wanted, to help Britain and thought that Canada might provide a way to do that without ruffling the isolationists whose focus was hemispheric, not purely American.

The common fear of all three countries, although never admitted publicly, was that Britain would be overrun and that its King and Fleet would have to flee to the Caribbean colonies and Canada. If that were to happen, North America itself could be threatened. While Roosevelt greatly admired Churchill's brave speeches to the British people, he worried that reality would not keep up with rhetoric. Unable to lead a direct American intervention, Roosevelt relied on Mackenzie King to communicate with Churchill.

The Canadian leader told Churchill in May 1940 that Roosevelt did not want to see the British fleet surrendered to the Germans. Instead, it should be sent to outlying territories of the Empire. If Germany attempted to starve Britain into returning its fleet to German control, then the United States would send food, under naval escort, to Britain and would be prepared to go to war if these ships were subject to German interference.[63] Churchill, although recognizing that the war might have to be fought from the outer reaches of the Empire, was nettled by Roosevelt's suggestions. The situation might work as the American had suggested, but only if the United States abandoned its neutrality.[64] When Roosevelt learned of these remarks from a Canadian emissary, he found them "alarming and distressing."[65] In their turn, the Canadians shared the British frustration with American unwillingness to sell them needed armaments. They did not realize that, in addition to the problems posed by the isolationists, the United States itself was not prepared.

A break came from an unofficial source. A group of American business, religious and newspaper men, members of New York's Century Club of which Roosevelt was also a member and calling themselves the Century Group, proposed on July 11, 1940, that the United States could trade destroyers, desperately needed by Britain, in return for bases in the Empire's territories in the Western Hemisphere.[66] This proposal was the origin of what would come to be known as "Lend Lease", a way of turning intervention in the European war into a sort of military-commercial deal, designed to buttress America's own defenses.

At a secret Washington meeting on July 10, Canadian military leaders had been disappointed by American reluctance to supply them weapons, even while the United States was interested in gaining bases in Eastern Canada and Newfoundland. The next day, the American attitude "appeared to have improved overnight,"[67] the Canadians reported. Perhaps there was a path toward the common objectives of the three governments. Canada supported Lend Lease, and Britain would ultimately agree to it.

None of these discussions had focused on the Pacific. The Japanese threat was much less urgent than the one that Germany posed to Britain itself. All three governments believed that the possibility of an attack on North America by the Germans and Italians by way of Iceland or Greenland was real and paid little attention at all to the possibility of a Japanese attack.

Mackenzie King and his staff wanted to do all they could to appeal to the Americans. So the road to Alaska emerged, unbidden by the United States. O.D. Skelton, the day-to-day head of Canada's Department of External Affairs and previously an opponent of the road, wrote in June 1940 to Mackenzie King, who also served as Minister of Foreign Affairs, that "serious consideration should be given to including construction of this road as an outstanding Canadian contribution to joint efforts for defence of the Pacific."[68] This message was followed up by one from Hugh Keenleyside, another high-ranking External Affairs official: "All available evidence seems to indicate that there is no economic justification for the construction of this road, but military and naval authorities in the United States have given strong evidence before Congressional committees as to its strategic value."[69] Canada's new-found zeal to attract American support could lead to the excesses of the Keenleyside memorandum, which obviously overstated the

position of the War and Navy Departments, still lukewarm
to the road.

Matters were moving toward a decision. Britain was
desperate for destroyers and tried to pressure Canada into
making public statements about munitions supply in order
to influence the Americans. Mackenzie King made his leanings clear in rejecting the suggestion: "I would not think of
doing so. It would help undo for the future any influence I
may have. Such a step would be in the nature of 'coercion'
— no wonder some diplomacies fail."[70]

The United States, still shackled by isolationism, was
emerging as a superpower whose great military and productive potential made its allies placate it and lean on it. Its
potential adversaries had not yet recognized the change nor
did they understand that they should begin to fear it. This
time, there would be no turning back inward for the United
States. How it dealt with both its friends and enemies would
begin to set the pattern for its continuing role as a superpower, no longer reluctant to lead in the world.

Roosevelt was scheduled to review Army maneuvers in
upstate New York on August 17, 1940, and invited Mackenzie King to meet with him there. Accompanied only by J.
Pierrepont Moffatt, the U.S. envoy to Canada, the Canadian
Prime Minister drove to Ogdensburg, N.Y. He arrived for
dinner, stunning Secretary of War Henry L. Stimson, who
had no idea that Roosevelt had planned such a meeting. The
President and the Prime Minister had privately cooked up a
summit that would forever change U.S.-Canadian relations.

At dinner, Roosevelt, Mackenzie King and Stimson
focused on the exchange of destroyers for Britain in return
for U.S. bases in Canada and elsewhere, a matter which the
President recognized was partly up to the Canadians. In
fact, Roosevelt said, that was the purpose of the meeting. He
proposed a joint board with military members and one lay
member from each side. While this board would be advisory, it would be responsible for defense planning for the
northern part of the Western Hemisphere, with the immediate focus on the northeastern coast of Canada. In making

recommendations, both countries would have equal weight.[71]

Mackenzie King was overwhelmed, never having dreamed that Roosevelt would go this far. Stimson, who took notes, gave a sense of the Canadian's distinctly undiplomatic reaction:

> Mackenzie King was perfectly delighted with the whole thing. He said, almost with tears in his eyes that the President's courage and initiative in bringing this out would be a most tremendous encouragement to the morale of Great Britain and Canada. He said he would at once agree to the creation of such a Board and that it should be done immediately. He again and again referred to the gratification which the British and he and Canada would feel on this subject.[72]

The idea had been Roosevelt's alone. He had not consulted the State, War or Navy Departments. In fact, these agencies did not share his interest in bases in Canada. On August 18, Roosevelt himself drafted the announcement, accepting Mackenzie King's suggestions that the body should be a "board" and that it should be "permanent".[73] Canada regarded the Ogdensburg "Agreement" as if it were a treaty, while Roosevelt refused to send the Ogdensburg "Declaration" to the Senate for ratification, so it has always remained in a kind of diplomatic limbo.

The media and public reaction in the United States, Canada and Britain was strongly favorable. Only one leader privately expressed skepticism — Winston Churchill. MacKenzie King had thought he had brought home a prize that the British Prime Minister would value, the promise of fifty destroyers. But Churchill disliked the notion of trading something to get them. This response served only to push Mackenzie King closer to the Americans, but he said nothing to Churchill. Perhaps realizing the weakness of his bargaining position, Churchill soon changed course and thanked Mackenzie King for what had been accomplished.[74]

The Permanent Joint Board on Defense — the PJBD — was quickly established. The American "lay" member would be the U.S. chairman, and Roosevelt appointed New York Mayor Fiorello H. LaGuardia to the position. Though technically a Republican, LaGuardia was a Roosevelt ally who had hoped to be made a Major General so that he could one day lead triumphant troops into Italy. But Roosevelt could not reward a New York Republican so highly. On August 26, just eight days after the Ogdensburg announcement, the PJBD met for the first time.

With one exception, the early PJBD meetings dealt only with the situation along the eastern seaboard, where enemy attack was considered possible. The exception was the Northwest Staging Route, a string of airfields planned and partially built by Canadian commercial interests supplemented by the federal government. These airfields would provide a direct route to Fairbanks, then the largest city in Alaska. In October 1940, the PJBD recommended that Canada develop the necessary airfields for military purposes as soon as possible. A formal recommendation was adopted the next month and funded by the Canadians in December.[75] The Northwest Staging Route would be the basis for all other joint defense projects in the Canadian West, but it would be the only one accomplished on a truly cooperative basis by the two governments.[76]

The Hyde Park Declaration of April 20, 1941 was a logical extension of Ogdensburg.[77] Roosevelt and Mackenzie King agreed to pool the defense production resources of the two countries to create an integrated supply. The Canadian was particularly pleased, because the United States looked to his country for major purchases, while Canadian purchases, on behalf of Britain, would be paid for by Lend Lease. The British High Commissioner to Canada, the Commonwealth equivalent of an ambassador, reported: "This is a declaration of love between Canada and the United States, and the bachelor Prime Minister who acted a proxy for the Dominion which is already married into the family of the British Commonwealth, is as proud and smiling as any infatuated swain."[78]

The proposed road to Alaska was an entirely different matter. At its November 1940 meeting, the PJBD agreed unanimously that its military value would be "negligible." During the following year, the Canadians began to get signs of American support; by July 1941 LaGuardia favored it,[79] not a position he likely would have taken without support from Washington.

After Pearl Harbor, Roosevelt moved toward a decision to build the road. On February 25-26, 1942, the PJBD met to consider the matter, which had virtually been decided by Roosevelt, and for which surveyors were already on the ground in Canada. The Canadians remained skeptical about the road's feasibility, its military need and its timeliness, because it was not due to be completed until January 1, 1944.[80] Even as events had moved toward a positive decision in Washington, the Canadian Chiefs of Staff said on February 4: "...we are of the opinion that the construction of this road by Canada is not warranted."[81]

The degree of the heightened American interest was demonstrated by the U.S. offer, made at the meeting, to assume the full responsibility for construction and its full cost. LaGuardia later reported to Roosevelt: "...we encountered more difficulty in giving 'something to somebody' than in collecting a war loan from an ally.... The Canadians...fear a terrific political backfire."[82]

Despite what clearly was Canadian opposition, the Canadian Section of the PJBD supported the recommendation "for reasons of general policy."[83] The general policy was that, if the United States wanted it badly enough to pay for it and Canada wanted to nurture its military alliance with the United States, Canada must acquiesce.[84] The Canadian members could not have been unaware of the steps already taken in Washington and Mackenzie King's willingness to allow the American surveyors into Canada.

The recommendation also settled the question of route A,B,C or D. It called for the road to follow the line of the Northwest Staging Route airfields, generally close to route C, which had fewer commercial and political advocates than the routes to the west. "I'm sure you will agree that all hell will break loose when our Washington and Oregon friends learn of the route,"[85] LaGuardia told Roosevelt. It did, but the plan, dictated by the military not the politicians, was not to be changed.[86]

The Canadian Government approved the recommendation on March 5. Mackenzie King understood well the real reason why Canada had been expected to make this decision. Later in March he confided in his diary that the road "was less intended for protection against the Japanese than as one of the fingers of the hand which America is placing more or less over the whole of the Western Hemisphere."[87]

Roosevelt initialed the PJBD recommendation with his "OK, FDR" on March 9, more than one month before Doolittle's raid, the same day as the first of 10,000 U.S. troops were arriving at the Alcan Highway site. The deal was done formally in an exchange of notes on March 17 and 18, 1942. The Americans would build and pay for the road, and the Canadians would provide the right of way and tax exemption. Six months after the war, the road would be turned over to Canada without charge. Canada would not agree to guarantee postwar access to the road by the U.S. military, and that proposed provision was dropped.[88]

What the Americans had first not wanted and then wanted ardently, they received from the Canadians mostly because they now wanted it so badly. From Mackenzie King's viewpoint, accepting the road, one of the rare times when members of the PJBD actually did not agree, was a small price to pay for Roosevelt's having allowed Canada to move out from under the shadow of Great Britain. The Canadian leader would have to keep earning his role, as was demonstrated by two events. In August 1941, a year after Ogdensburg, Roosevelt had met with Churchill aboard naval vessels anchored off the coast of Newfoundland, technically not a part of Canada. Roosevelt knew that he would offend Mackenzie King by not inviting him to this meeting. The Canadian was not happy. In another offensive incident, a Northwest Airlines plane landed without permission in

Edmonton, Alberta, on February 27, 1942. Operating under contract with the Army Air Corps, the plane was seen as a attempt to gain an advantage for the postwar airline business in the Canadian West. Canada seized, then released, the plane, but made angrily clear its sensitivity about its sovereignty.[89]

Freed by Pearl Harbor from the shackles of isolationism, Roosevelt was leading the United States into its role as a superpower on many fronts; its relations with Canada were a textbook for how it would proceed in the future, even after the end of the war. The United States would use bilateral and multilateral arrangements to cast its actions in a cooperative rather than a coercive mode. It would spend its own money and deploy its productive capacity abroad if necessary to gain its objectives. It would not acquire new territory, just the use of it.

Add to this policy the indisputable charm and self-confidence of F.D.R. to say nothing of American power, and the allies, beginning with Mackenzie King's Canada, could not resist. Ogdensburg, now lost in the obscurity of history, was one of the first steps of the emerging American superpower.

CHAPTER 3.

FROM ISOLATIONISM TO MULTILATERALISM

Things change. The United States had purchased Russian America from the czarist regime, and Russian America had become Alaska. The czars' rule had become the Communists' Dictatorship of the Proletariat, and Russia had become the core of the Union of Soviet Socialist Republics. Most, but not all, Americans did not like socialism, and they hated communism.

In 1933, Roosevelt agreed to open diplomatic relations with the U.S.S.R., a step which his three Republican predecessors had refused. But the relationship was barely cordial. Americans feared the professed desire of the Soviets to extend their system across the world, a threat that seemed possible because of the despair caused by the Great Depression. The Soviets understood that the United States hoped for and had even promoted the end of their totalitarian rule. Traditional Russian suspicion of outsiders was only heightened by Soviet wariness about American intentions.

In 1939, the Soviet Union had signed a nonaggression pact with the Nazi regime. The Nazis did not hide their hatred of the Soviets, but wanted to be able to direct all of their military efforts to the conquest of Western Europe. The Soviets also wanted to buy time to prepare for the ultimate war with Germany, so the cynical deal was struck. The parties to the nonaggression pact proceeded immediately to attack aggressively and occupy the lands that lay between them and created a temporary buffer zone.

The Japanese, who had faced off against the Soviets over Mongolia, dropped their plans for military action there, once the Soviet-German pact was concluded. In April, 1941, Japan and the Soviet Union signed a nonaggression treaty, allowing the Japanese to concentrate its attentions on the Americans and the Soviets to prepare for war with Germany.

Both treaties embodied the triumph of expediency over principle. The Americans, clinging to neutrality in the face of this old diplomatic game, scorned all the players.

On June 22, 1941, the old game took a new, but not unexpected, turn. Despite having been warned that the Germans were now ready to invade, the Soviet Union suffered severe losses from a huge, surprise attack launched in the middle of the night. Just before the start of Germany's Operation Barbarossa, the Red Air Force had 7,700 aircraft in western Russia, including some of the newest designs. The German Luftwaffe had only 1,940 planes. But the Soviets were caught with their planes on the ground, just as would the Americans at Pearl Harbor a few months later. At the end of the day, the German air force had destroyed 1,811 Red Air Force planes, while the Luftwaffe had lost only 35 aircraft. And that was just the beginning. Within the first week, 4,017 Soviet planes were destroyed at the cost of only 150 German aircraft.[90] The Soviets were retreating headlong toward Moscow, trading land for time.

The Soviets did not at first know how the Americans would react. On June 26, the State Department informed Soviet Ambassador Constantine Oumansky in Washington that the U.S. would provide aid.[91] The transformation in American official policy had taken only four days. Here was one of clearest cases ever of one of the basic rules of foreign policy: my enemy's enemy is my friend. Churchill, acting at the same time to provide help, was brutally honest, saying: "If Hitler invaded Hell [I] would at least make a favorable reference to the Devil."[92]

The United States, worried about the speed of German advances, sought assurances that the Soviet Union could survive. This concern reflected no more positive thinking about Communism, but the belief that if the U.S.S.R. could stop the Germans and engage them in protracted and bitter battle, the Atlantic powers could gather the strength to open the second front. Before pouring aid into the Soviet Union, the United States needed to know if it was worth making the investment. In August 1941, presidential confidant Harry Hopkins, just back from Moscow reported that the Soviets could hold on, but needed massive military aid.

Even before Hopkins' report, a new role for the Northwest Staging Route, the chain of airfields being built between Montana and Alaska, was emerging. Originally, the PJBD had found that it was needed for the defense of Alaska. Now, it might be used to help supply the Soviet Union. At the end of June 1941, Oumansky told U.S. officials that the Soviet Union needed 3,000 fighters and the same number of bombers. Some of the bombers could fly from Alaska to Siberia, where the airfields were in excellent condition, he said.[93]

Events seemed to be moving quickly. On August 31, 1941, without any advance warning, two Soviet flying boats suddenly appeared off the coast of Alaska and were escorted to a safe landing at Nome. The planes carried more than 40 airmen, determined to move on to the lower 48 states to begin their training on U.S. bombers.[94] No agreement yet existed between the United States and the Soviet Union, and problems began to emerge almost immediately.

The Soviet general in charge of the surprise visitors did not like American B-25 bombers and went directly to Washington to demand B-17s, the new "Flying Fortresses." The Army Air Corps refused on the grounds that they were not suited to Soviet combat support needs. The Soviets haggled some more, first accepting and then rejecting B-26s. They doubted that B-25s, which they finally accepted, could make the long flight by way of Alaska, so they insisted that the first five, sent in November, should travel by ship.[95] The Alaska route had been symbolically opened by two round trips of the flying boats, but the actual transfer of war planes would take another year to begin.

Why did a country, still reeling from the German invasion, having suffered major losses of aircraft and urgently seeking American aid, delay delivery and haggle over the help it desperately needed? Why did U.S. envoys have to travel to Moscow for high-level meetings to see how aid could be provided, almost having to beg the Soviets to accept help and the use of the Alaska route?

The answer was partly contained in a later report by Gen. John R. Deane, head of the U.S. military mission to Moscow during much of the war: "Soviet officials have an inherent distrust of foreigners and may be expected to examine for hidden motives any proposal for collaboration. This will always result in indeterminate delays...."[96] Just as LaGuardia found, it was sometimes difficult to "give something to somebody."

The Soviets were preoccupied by the concept of a second front. At the same time as they were urging Britain to launch an attack on the European continent, a refrain that would be heard from almost the moment of the Barbarossa attack until D-Day, the Soviets wanted to avoid a second front on their Asian flank. Both the Americans and Soviets considered the U.S.S.R.-Japan treaty to be quite fragile, especially because of their common lack of information about the Japanese war potential. For the Soviets, these doubts meant that they should give as little cause for concern as possible to the Japanese. For the Americans, such concerns called for increased preparedness, a conclusion obviously acted upon at Pearl Harbor where the Pacific fleet assembled.

These concerns were compounded by Russia's historical distrust of all foreigners. Responding to Oumansky, the War Department asked for "information on all Trans-Siberian airfields and their weather reporting and communications facilities."[97] The United States never got the answer, and Soviet suspicion seemed to increase simply because the questions had been asked.

In September, W. Averill Harriman, responsible for Lend Lease aid to Britain, went to Moscow and raised the possibility of supplying aircraft from Alaska across Siberia. Joseph Stalin, the Communist leader, showed initial interest, but promptly balked when Harriman mentioned that American airmen could ferry aircraft across Siberia. Suddenly, Stalin found the Alaska route too dangerous. For the time being, the planes would be moved by ship through the treacherous North Sea or around Africa or by air over it. All of these routes would stretch delivery from a few days to many weeks.

The Soviet position was obviously meant to keep Americans off of Soviet soil and not just for historical reasons. Stalin feared that the United States would use Siberia as a base for direct attacks on Japan. If the Soviets conceded this point, they would hand Japan a pretext for war. Beyond that, Oumansky, soon to be replaced in Washington, had gone too far in saying that the Siberian airfields were ready for use. While it would take years to bring them up even to the standards of the Northwest Staging Route, it would take many months for them even to be usable.

As Roosevelt grew more concerned about the possibility of a Japanese attack, which would soon materialize in the Japanese occupation of Kiska and Attu in the Aleutians in June 1942, he came to believe that the Soviet Union itself might soon come under attack by Japan. He tried to sell Stalin on the idea that if Americans delivered planes to Siberia, they could readily be diverted to landing fields near Vladivostok, permitting the "the United States quickly [to come to] the assistance of the Soviet Union."[98] Stalin promptly replied that the planes could come across Siberia, but saying: "As to whose pilots should fly the planes from Alaska, it seems to me that can be assigned to...Soviet airmen."[99]

With that matter apparently settled, Stalin then became impatient for the early opening of the route. But the United States would not send planes without a preliminary survey of the Siberian airfields. After first arguing that the survey would be conducted only by Soviet personnel, Moscow military leaders backed down when the Americans insisted on a joint crew. For one time only, Americans flew from Alaska across Siberia. The American survey leader reported somewhat optimistically that the route, although primitive, could be used.[100]

Ultimately, the Alaska-Siberia route would be the prime route of supply, simply because it made the most sense. Only about 30 percent of the planes were making it across the North Sea to Murmansk.[101] The success ratio across Siberia promised to exceed 90 percent.

This Lend Lease supply to the Soviets involved two of the war's most unusual situations. First, the United States was actually opening its own second front against Hitler by sending troops and supplies to Europe across the Bering Sea as well as across the Atlantic. And, just as the Americans would "invade" Canada and many other friendly countries, the Soviet were coming to Fairbanks to set up military operations on American soil.

Despite the bleak outlook at the start of the war and their dependence on others, the Soviets insisted on maintaining their new empire and keeping their distance from the United States, the only possible challenge to them in the future. In sharp contrast, Britain sought the American embrace, with a growing awareness that it was approaching the demise of its own empire.

Britain had long been involved in a kind of mating dance with the United States with the goal of bringing the Americans fully into the war against Germany and Italy. Despite his oratorical bravado ("give us the tools and we will finish the job"), Churchill knew that Britain could only win the war with full-scale U.S. participation.[102]

But he understood that isolationist sentiment in the United States prevented Roosevelt from excessively overt actions and certainly from full participation.

In the meantime, Britain and its Commonwealth stood alone. As a later report stated: "Canada, her war effort now steadily expanding on a wide front, was for the moment the United Kingdom's most powerful ally, and her growing military force in Britain had been an important factor in British defensive calculations when invasion seemed imminently threatened in the autumn [of 1940]."[103] But Britain, Canada and the others clearly did not have the forces "to finish the job."

Churchill's first reaction to Ogdensburg may have been concern that Canada's attention was being diverted by the Americans, while his second, more favorable, reaction seemed to be the realization that Canada was drawing the United States closer to support and intervention, just as Mackenzie King had thought. Churchill was perceptive enough to recognize that Canada's first obligation would be its own defense and that its direct relationship with the United States would be crucial.

Pearl Harbor provided Churchill with a bittersweet moment. The Americans were now in the war. "So we had won after all,"[104] he would write. But he also worried that the war in the Pacific might now get higher priority than the war in Europe, especially in light of Roosevelt's call on December 8 only for a declaration of war against Japan. He had thought he had a commitment from Roosevelt to give Europe priority, but that was before the sneak attack at Pearl Harbor. Berlin and Rome provided him some reassurance when, on December 11, 1941, honoring their treaty with Tokyo, they declared war on the United States. Still, on December 12, Churchill set out across the Atlantic to meet with Roosevelt in Washington and, incidentally, with Mackenzie King.

Canada, which had declared war on Germany in 1939 after waiting a week following Britain's declaration, reacted to Pearl Harbor by declaring war on Japan even before the United States did. Canadians recognized that Canada was no longer engaged simply as Britain's prime backer, but was in serious danger itself. This changed perception ended the dichotomy in Ottawa between those clinging to Britain and those gravitating toward the United States. Churchill would quickly come to understand that change.

In Washington, Churchill fell in behind Roosevelt's plan to create the allied coalition, which the President called the United Nations. Mackenzie King came to Washington in late December to take part in the discussions, and Churchill spent the last three days of 1941 in Ottawa, where he delivered another of his rousing wartime speeches. Then, he went back to Washington to join Roosevelt on January 1, 1942, in the declaration of the United Nations.

Just as Canada now moved in behind American wartime leadership, so did Churchill. The United Nations now included Britain and its Dominions, China, the Soviet Union, European governments in exile and a collection of Latin American countries, which had declared war on the Axis. "What the [United Nations] ceremony and the declaration did, without formal proclamation, was to accept Washington's position as the imperial capital of the Allied war effort, although with Stalin maintaining a semi-independent position as Emperor of the East,"[105] said Roy Jenkins in his Churchill biography.

Overall, Churchill was pleased, because he had obtained the agreement that, notwithstanding Pearl Harbor, the United States would give first priority to the defeat of Germany. Roosevelt obviously thought that Hitler pulled the strings of Italy and Japan and that the way to win the war was to cut off the Axis' head. After the Battle of Midway in mid-1943, the Pacific war would turn more rapidly than Roosevelt had thought it would, but for now the emphasis in the Pacific would be on defense.

In effect, then, the agreement that the United Nations should fight primarily in Europe, so desperately sought by Churchill, meshed with efforts by the United States and Canada to develop defenses on the West Coast and in Alaska. The relationship between the two North American nations had never been close, but now they would draw together for their common defense. In its ability to dictate the war's priorities, the United States had moved in less than a month from isolationism to world leadership.

Leadership in war depends on strength. In 1937, the American armed forces had ranked below Portugal's in the list of world powers. Even then, all Americans, isolationist or interventionist, were beginning to acknowledge that the United States would have to deal with a radically changed world order, created mainly by Hitler's Germany. The isolationists recognized the need to defend the Western Hemisphere; the interventionists wanted to confront Hitler directly. Both supported an expansion of the armed forces.

In September 1938 at Munich, Britain and France had averted war with Germany by conceding to Hitler the right to occupy large parts of Czechoslovakia. While British Prime Minister Neville Chamberlain may have thought that Munich had bought "peace in our time," even neutral Washington was highly skeptical. Two months later, the expansion of the U.S. Army began.

By the spring of 1940, with the end of the "sitzkrieg", the "phony war" that had followed Germany's 1939 attack on Poland, Roosevelt stepped up the pace of the gradual increases in the size of the Army. In June 1940, France fell. In August 1940, the President federalized the National Guard, and its personnel began moving onto active duty. In September, Selective Service — the draft — was enacted, although the isolationists won approval of a provision that would limit the use of draftees to the Western Hemisphere, unless Congress had declared war.

By December 7, 1941, the Army had 1,647,477 troops, about ten times as many as three years earlier.[106] The United States was not unprepared, though it had been disastrously surprised. Its military strength, already great and still growing, gave it the undeniable right to the leadership it now assumed.

The United Nations, the expansion of the American defense perimeter far from U.S. shores, a more vigilant defense of Hawaii, the new link to Alaska and a defense establishment that would not be allowed to shrivel in peacetime were all lessons learned in reacting to Pearl Harbor. The American people could be "very certain that this form of treachery shall never again endanger us," Roosevelt had promised in his Declaration of War speech, "by abandoning, for once and for all, the illusion that we can ever again isolate ourselves from the rest of humanity."[107] This was the President's own declaration of war against the isolationism that had caused the United States to refuse to join the League of Nations after World War I and had kept it from preparing for the inevitable war now upon it. The Japanese attack had literally been a wake-up call, and the President, Congress and the people believed that, if these lessons were taken to heart, this war would be the last time that America would have to worry about homeland defense.

So they thought.

PART II. ALCAN AND THE "AMERICAN DILEMMA"

CHAPTER 4.

THE ARMY OF TOMORROW

Neither as dramatic nor as risky as Doolittle's raid, the Alcan Highway would takes its place in history as the first major deployment of ground forces of the U.S. in the war. The Army's decision to build the Alcan Highway as quickly as possible forced the Alcan projects to confront the oldest and most divisive issue in American history — the treatment of Americans of African origin by the government. The Civil War had brought an end of slavery, but a monumental study by Gunnar Myrdal, a Swedish economist and sociologist, entitled *An American Dilemma*, would reveal that the United States in the 1940s had not found a way for the black and white races to live together much less fight a war together.

When Brig. Gen William M. Hoge, in charge of Alcan Highway construction, arrived in the Yukon, he quickly concluded that the four Engineer regiments assigned to building the road could not get the job done in time to defend Alaska and support Lend Lease deliveries. He asked for more troops. Thanks to the draft, the Army had already assembled some trained units available to respond almost immediately. Among the Engineers, the pool from which road builders could be drawn, were "colored" Engineer General Service regiments, recently converted from so-called "separate" labor battalions. The remainder of the troops that Hoge would receive, three additional regiments, would be black.

The pioneer road, a rough road through the bush to be built at top speed allowing supplies to get to Alaska and providing the path for a more permanent road, would be built by seven regiments, four white and three black. About 34 percent of the 10,756 enlisted personnel were members of the three black regiments.[108] In the U.S. Army of the 21st Century, about 28 percent of the enlisted personnel is black. So the Alcan forces might look, to today's casual observer, as if it were the Army of tomorrow. But they were not. They were a despised, segregated afterthought.

Yet Alcan would be an important point along the path toward integration. The Alcan road project would represent one of the rare times that American blacks and whites, similarly supplied, would perform the same tasks under the same conditions in isolation from the rest of the world, thus making it possible for blacks and whites to compare themselves.

Just as it was in the case of Alcan, the long history of American use of blacks in the military was characterized by initial white resistance to their participation, then agreement to their involvement as a military necessity in time of crisis. There had been no black soldiers in the Continental Army until volunteer enlistments dropped and about five thousand blacks were allowed to serve in the Revolutionary War.[109] Even during the Civil War, the Union Army did not include blacks until Lincoln felt himself ready to confront sensitivities in the border states, well after he had issued the Emancipation Proclamation in January 1863.[110]

The post-war, reconstructionist Congress was ready to reward blacks for their service and created by law two black cavalry regiments and two black infantry regiments. These troops served in the West and fought alongside Col. Theodore Roosevelt's Rough Riders at San Juan Hill. But Roosevelt, as president, set their cause back immeasurably. After an alleged riot by black troops resentful of their treatment by white civilians in Brownsville, Texas, he dishonorably discharged three companies without listening to their side of the story. His biographer would comment that "Brownsville had been proof to many, and perhaps even a warning to himself, of the truth of Lord Acton's famous dictum [power corrupts; absolute power corrupts absolutely]."[111] The President had made a monstrous mistake, as it turned out, but the stigma stuck. The small degree of integration that had taken place by the time of the Spanish-American War was gone.

When the United States could no longer avoid entry into World War I, black Americans sought to join the armed forces. Once in the Army, they faced the most crude racism. In one incident, when a black soldier protested illegal segregation in a civilian facility, his commanding officer, admitting he was right, issued an order finding the man to be "guilty of the greater wrong in doing anything, no matter how legally correct, that would provoke race animosity."[112]

Aside from the routine racism they encountered in the Army, blacks would remember two celebrated cases, which characterized the entire experience. In June 1917, Col. Charles Young, one of the first three black graduates of West Point and the highest ranking black Army officer, was forcibly retired on the grounds of high blood pressure. In protest and to demonstrate his fitness, he rode on horseback from Ohio to Washington, D.C. The Army was not ready to promote him to general officer, which would have entailed combat responsibilities and possibly the leadership of white troops. The second case was the creation of the obviously undertrained and unskilled 92nd Division, composed of black troops. From its formation, the black press said that "the Ninety-second Division is bound to be a failure as a unit organization. Is it possible that persons in the War Department wish this division to be a failure?"[113]

In sharp contrast, the four regiments of the 93rd Division, also composed of black troops, were placed under French command and integrated into their forces. Three of the regiments and a company of the fourth were awarded the Croix de Guerre, despite the fact that the U.S. Army had warned French officers not to mingle with or commend the black troops.[114] News coverage of these and other black American troops, especially those in combat, was favorable. But awards and news stories were superficial recognition that did not assuage the effects of racist discrimination. General Robert Lee Bullard, Commander of the Second Army, which included the 92nd Division, wrote: "Poor Negroes! They are hopelessly inferior."[115]

Many of the Army officers were from the South. In the aftermath of the Civil War, the Southern economy would take most of a century to recover and provided only limited opportunities for economic advancement for rising young men. The Union restored, they could join the Army and qualify as officers. Not only did the Army have what seemed to be a disproportionate number of Southern officers, but they were often assigned to lead black troops. Northern officers might not have had much contact with blacks, but Southerners "understood" them, the Army thought. What many, but certainly not all, Southerners "understood" was how to perpetuate traditional racism.

In the face of this open racism and resistance to their participation, why did blacks fight so hard for the right to serve in the armed forces? They believed in the American dream. In an analysis of World War I participation, one observer summed it up: "American Negroes had hoped that in making the world safe for democracy the United States would grant more democracy to its largest minority."[116]

After the war, blacks discovered there had been no gains in their quest for democracy. The number of lynchings increased each year, and many of the victims were "soldiers still in uniform."[117] Race riots broke out when blacks were no longer willing to accept their fate at the hands of racist attackers.

In the interwar period, the Army devised plan after unexecuted plan for using black troops. The generals drew up these plans with no joy. In fact, their logic was fundamentally racist: "To follow the policy of exempting the negro population from combat service means that the white population, upon which the future of the country depends, would suffer the brunt of loss, the negro population, none; the rising white generation 34 percent, and the rising negro population, nothing."[118] In other words, blacks should be killed at the same rate as whites so as to prevent them from becoming a larger part of the population. Once having swallowed this seemingly bitter pill, the Army found that black regiments, nothing smaller, could serve alongside white regiments.

Planning was one thing, but peace imposed a new reality: the reduction in the size of the armed forces. Instead of building new black units, those already in existence were depleted. There was now no room for them. The only way a black could join the Regular Army was to identify a vacancy, travel to the post where it existed at his own expense and enlist. As for West Point, only one black, Benjamin O. Davis, Jr., the future commander of the Tuskegee airmen, graduated between 1920 and 1940. On the eve of a new World War, nothing had changed from 1918. No plan could be carried out, because military commanders continued to believe that blacks, not just black soldiers, were inferior to whites. Stereotypes were rampant in official military studies: "the negro...has a musical nature and a marked sense of rhythm."[119]

War was coming. The Army's sorry past history and the increased expectations created by FDR's social policies called for change. In fact, since Brownsville, nothing had changed. The participation of blacks in the Army, especially in combat units, was a matter of political and social concern, but not really of any relevance to the Army. The record strongly suggests that, on the eve of World War II, most military leaders would have preferred to do without the services of American blacks, if it could have been accomplished without political upheaval.

But politics in America had changed. The disastrous Depression had given Roosevelt the opportunity to build a coalition of those who had suffered from past policies, and his political success depended in part on support from the black community. Mindful of their new political clout and at the boiling point, at least in the North, over the kind of persistent official racism demonstrated by the Army, black leaders were now ready to engage in an open and sustained struggle for equal treatment. For the first time in the battle over participation in the armed forces, black leaders moved from being deferential to being confrontational.

The black press, composed of hundreds of weekly newspapers reaching millions of readers but largely unknown to white America, launched the Double V campaign for victory over fascism abroad and racism at home. Jim Crow was just as much the enemy as Adolf Hitler. As the black newspapers became increasing militant, the campaign reached the broad black public. In the words of one historian, this increase in demands for equality and the more insistent tone of these demands "might well mark the beginning of the modern civil rights movement".[120]

Franklin D. Roosevelt had extended New Deal social programs to all Americans, regardless of race, and for that the black community was grateful. He sought to maintain a broad political coalition that, while welcoming traditionally Republican black support, would not offend the "Solid South," the core of reliably Democratic states that gave him the presidency and the Democrats control of Congress. While attempting to placate black leaders, he would not confront or challenge the racist attitudes of Southern senators and congressmen. Meanwhile, Eleanor Roosevelt openly supported civil rights, and her advocacy could bring political benefits to her husband without compromising his coalition.

While black demands called for greater democracy across the United States, meaning more political and economic opportunity for blacks, the nascent civil rights movement would focus first on the military, especially the Army, which would have the greatest need for added manpower. For the first time, the movement would not merely demand equality, but integration.

The mobilization plans of the interwar period were pushed aside as war loomed, and Congress proceeded to consider the Selective Service Act. It looked like the Civil War all over again. Northerners proposed that anti-discrimination provisions be included in the Act. The Southern

Senate potentates would not countenance actual integration. Senator John H. Overton, Democrat of Louisiana, told the hearings: "If we should undertake to establish mixed units in the Army, it would be subversive to discipline, subversive to morale, and would not be of benefit either to the colored or to the white race."[121] Discussion ended.

In its final form the Selective Service Act banned discrimination and was predicated on the Army's assurance that blacks would be drafted in proportion to their percentage of the population, about 10 percent. But the law contained two troublesome provisions. No man would be inducted whose physical or mental fitness was unacceptable and unless there were adequate housing and related facilities. The first left the armed services to exclude draftees at their discretion, and the second, because of the need for segregated facilities, could limit the number of black soldiers.

Roosevelt told his cabinet just before the passage of the Act that he was "troubled" by the claims of black representatives that "their race under the draft was limited to labor battalions." At Marshall's urging, the Army informed the President that blacks would get "proportionate shares in all branches of the Army, in the proper ratio to the population — approximately 10 percent."[122]

Slippage began immediately. The Act was approved on September 16, 1940, and the War Department issued a press release that same day announcing that nine percent of the first draft call would be blacks. It also noted that "the creation of additional colored combat organizations is now under consideration."[123]

Neither the law nor this statement satisfied black leaders. The promise to ban discrimination would do nothing to end segregation and, in fact, Roosevelt had never promised that. The policy of "separate, but equal" embodied in the famous 1896 Supreme Court decision in *Plessy v. Ferguson*[124] continued. Blacks and whites understood that the decision had guaranteed separate facilities for the races, but had produced no equality, and black spokesmen held out no hope for the Army now. The statement that black combat units were "under consideration" gave faint hope that the percentage of blacks in all branches of the military would reflect their proportion of the eligible population. They had been virtually excluded from the Air Corps, and this promise was not likely to improve that situation. Black soldiers would once again be assigned mostly to service units.

The President met on September 27, 1940, with Walter F. White, head of the NAACP, T. Arnold Hill of the National Urban League and A. Philip Randolph, President of the Brotherhood of Sleeping Car Porters, the only labor union headed by a black. Roosevelt was accompanied by Secretary of the Navy Frank Knox and Assistant Secretary of War Robert P. Patterson. In effect, this was a summit meeting, arranged at White's request by Mrs. Roosevelt, at which both sides would try to find a way for blacks to participate in the armed forces without continuing conflict. It was a major event in the early civil rights movement.

White and his colleagues advocated integration and the use of blacks in all branches with special attention to the Air Corps and the Navy. To be practical, White suggested that black regiments or even smaller units should be assigned to serve under the same commands as similar white units, which could become a step toward fully unsegregated units.[125] Patterson made vague promises about calling black officers to active duty, Knox rejected any increased use of blacks, and the President said he would contact the black leaders after further talks with government people.

On October 8, 1940, Patterson gave the President a policy statement, meant to respond to the black leaders' demands. The memo accepted the principle of proportional participation, with black units "in each major branch of the service." The current aviation training given blacks would be accelerated. But the memo rejected integration: "The policy of the War department is not to intermingle colored and white enlisted personnel in the same regimental organizations." It also said that white officers would continue to lead black units.[126] The President wrote "O.K. F.D.R." on

THE ARMY OF TOMORROW

the document, and it became the policy applied, more or less, throughout the war.

The next day, Stephen Early, the President's press secretary, sent the policy to the Democratic National Committee and suggested that it be given wide dissemination in the black press. Early implied that the policy had met the approval of the black leaders who had participated in the September 27 meeting. In fact, they had never heard from the President nor had any advance knowledge of the press release. But, after its release, they were strongly attacked in the black press. To the black leaders, Early's statement looked like a crude attempt to trap them into supporting the policy, and they protested. They knew the provision relating to aviation training was untrue; no such training was being given, and blacks were being rejected when they applied. Proportional participation was already included under Selective Service. And they certainly did not condone a policy rejecting integration. They released the memo they had handed to the President in order to show that they did not agree with the policy.

The press release came just one month before the presidential election in which Roosevelt sought an unprecedented third term. Wendell Willkie, his Republican opponent, had taken a position much more closely aligned with the black leadership. The President realized that the October 9 press release had backfired, and done more harm with black leaders and media. Under pressure from Roosevelt, a reluctant Early corrected his statement. Even more had to be done to demonstrate Roosevelt's sensitivity to black demands, although he would never go so far as to support integration, for the political cost of such a policy change in the South would be too great.

The Army responded by committing itself to a specific number of blacks to be trained in the Air Corps and the formation a new black cavalry brigade. Roosevelt had to go still further. On October 25, as the election loomed, he nominated Col. Benjamin O. Davis, the highest-ranking black Army officer, to the rank of brigadier general, the first black general officer in American history. That same day, Secretary of War Stimson appointed William Hastie, a former federal judge in the Virgin Islands and the Dean of the Howard University Law School, as his Civilian Aide on Negro Affairs.

A short time earlier, Roosevelt had promoted scores of colonels over Davis on the promotion list, so his nomination bore the clear stamp of political pandering. *Time* magazine not only pointed out that Davis might end up commanding white soldiers, a violation of the policy announced earlier in the month, but suggested that Davis could simply retire the next year. "By then the election will be over,"[127] it said. Either *Time* had forgotten the Young affair just before World War I or it thought that, having gulled the blacks, the President would suffer little harm if he dumped Davis after the election. The Davis appointment was generally popular with blacks, but he never commanded any troops.

As for Secretary Stimson, he openly regarded the appointment as purely political. He wrote that "I had a good deal of fun with Knox over the necessity that he was facing of appointing a colored Admiral and a battle fleet full of colored sailors ... and I told him that when I called next time at the Navy Department with my colored Brigadier General I expected to be met with the colored Admiral."[128] Stimson was fond of reminding people of his abolitionist background.

The Hastie appointment created a more complex situation than did Davis's. From the Army's viewpoint, Stimson was merely following the path of his World War I predecessor who had appointed a black aide to act as liaison with the black community, essentially a public relations position. Hastie wanted to play a larger role, yet did not want to be seen simply as a black advocate. Stimson's appointment letter said that his duties were "to assist in the formulation, development and administration of policies looking to the fair and effective utilization of Negroes in all branches of the military service."[129] Hastie believed that he could show the War Department that better treatment of blacks would produce better military results.

While the War Department apparently believed that Hastie would be snowed under dealing with individual complaints from black soldiers, office visits and tours of facilities, the Judge saw his duties principally to be the "general task of facilitating the equitable integration of the Negro into so much of the National Defense Program as falls within the jurisdiction of the War Department."[130] He prepared recommendations and reviewed many proposals relating to black troops, and after he complained that he received the proposals at a stage in their development when he would have no influence, Army chiefs were directed to send such policy matters to him "for comment or concurrence before final action."[131]

As Hastie began his work, the black leaders became increasingly frustrated with Roosevelt, who had won the votes of most blacks in November 1940. In January 1941, Randolph proposed the March on Washington, 10,000 blacks demanding employment opportunity and equal treatment in the armed forces. The proposal received so much support that Randolph upped the call to 50,000 people to march on July 1. Roosevelt was alarmed and anxious to prevent the March and once again asked the military to respond to the demands for integration. The Army continued to oppose "mingling" in the military, but could see the need for some kind of action on employment discrimination. The President tried to satisfy the black leaders by calling for defense contractors not to discriminate in employment. Still, the March was not called off. On June 18, 1941, White and Randolph met with the President. He had now shifted to dealing only with the issue of defense contractors and, under great pressure, offered to issue an executive order creating the Fair Employment Practices Committee. Randolph agreed to call off the March, and immediately faced the charge by the Negro newspapers that the deal was a "sellout", because nothing had been done about the military.[132]

The March on Washington Movement was the start of black mass militancy. The interest it had engendered and the persistent demands of the black press meant things would never be the same again; blacks would not blindly support the war effort.

At the same time, Hastie began to be ignored by the War Department. He was not informed of the opening of segregated facilities or their relocation after whites protested. Papers began to circulate with the notation "Not to be shown to Judge Hastie" and he was prevented from commenting on a request for information on black morale, leaving the way open for a draft report saying: "Those Negro leaders who seek to prove discrimination because of color employ special pleading for a race which as a class, has not as yet the attained mental equipment to be employed in military functions other than those where brawn is a prerequisite."[133] Much of this language was deleted in the final report, but the thinking persisted.

Hastie prepared his own survey and recommendations in September 1941. He began his survey with a direct assault: "The traditional mores of the South have been widely accepted and adopted as the basis of policy and practice affecting the Negro soldier...." The Judge found that only five percent of the Army were blacks and that blacks were excluded from combat and other functions on the grounds that they were not intelligent enough. Instead of an analysis of why blacks did not do as well as whites on tests, he argued that, whatever their test results, many blacks could carry out combat tasks. He called for integration "[a]t some place in the armed services."[134]

Stimson assigned General Marshall to prepare the War Department's reply. On December 1, 1941, Marshall provided a memo notable in the Army of that day for its lack of overt racist sentiment. Instead, Marshall focused on the practical realities as he saw them:

> The problems presented with reference to utilizing negro personnel in the Army should be faced squarely. In doing so, the following facts must be

recognized; first, that the War Department cannot ignore the social relationships between negroes and whites which has (sic) been established by the American people through custom and habit; second, that either through lack of educational opportunities or other causes the level of intelligence and occupational skill of the negro population is considerably below that of the white; third, the Army will attain its maximum strength only if its personnel is properly placed in accordance with the capabilities of individuals; and fourth, that experiments within the Army in the solution of social problems are fraught with danger to efficiency, discipline and morale. [135]

In effect, he agreed with Hastie, that the mores of the South, its custom and habit, had created social relationships not to be ignored and that personnel should be used in accordance with individual capabilities, a concept that could logically lead to integration. But, Marshall concluded, the Army at war was no place for social "experiments." In other words, as had been the response throughout the interwar period to requests for increased use of blacks: not here, not now.

Though he was unwilling to challenge the Army's pervasive racism, Marshall was a leader with class, and the Army might have perhaps fared better if it had adhered to his argument. Instead of the difficult sentiment he expressed, it would continue to promise more to blacks than it had any intention of providing.

While Marshall was drafting his response, Hastie and the public affairs staff were setting up a high-level conference of black editors and publishers, a kind of military "show and tell" that was scheduled for December 8, 1941. General Marshall was to speak to the group and would have to address the message contained in the Hastie recommendations. That the meeting, taking place on the day that America declared war on Japan, was not postponed provides a measure of the significance attached to the problem of black participation in the war effort.

Marshall said that the Army was making progress on its promises and announced, for the first time, that a black division was being considered. He admitted that the War Department was not satisfied with progress so far. "And I am not personally satisfied with it either,"[136] he added. His personal remark was almost electrifying, coming as it did at a moment of high emotion. However, an hour later, an officer read a statement to the group saying: "The Army is not a sociological laboratory" and rejected "[e]xperiments to meet the wishes and demands of the champions of every race and creed for the solution of their problems...."[137] The champions of the black race to whom these remarks were addressed, hoped that Marshall was moving their way and feared that nothing would change. Their hopes would be denied, their fears rewarded.

In fact, the situation was deteriorating, and Hastie knew it. Despite the policy announced in 1940, the Army was not distributing black troops to all branches. "Generally, plans for utilization of Negro soldiers still reflect a prevailing view in the Army that as small a number of Negroes as possible be given combat training,"[138] the Judge wrote early in 1942.

Stimson and Patterson were coming increasingly to see Hastie as an NAACP agitator, not willing to sell the War Department program to the black community, and they were undoubtedly right that he saw himself more as an advocate than as an advisor. Stimson established an Advisory Committee on Negro Troop Policies, headed by Assistant Secretary of War John J. McCloy, a white. General Davis was a member, but Hastie, who had not even been informed of its creation, was excluded. The Committee would accomplish little.

Then Hastie learned that the Air Corps, unlike all other branches which had integrated Officer Candidate Schools, planned to set up a separate OCS for blacks. In January 1943, he resigned. The Army backed off the OCS plan and appointed a less militant successor to Hastie. The 1944 election and the desperate need for manpower would bring some changes, but the treatment and use of blacks remained fundamentally what it had been in World War I: Southern-style discrimination.

In order to try to keep the promise of proportional participation at least in the Army as a whole, Selective Service used a quota system, which had to be continually calibrated to take into account changes caused by voluntary enlistments. The Army resisted Selective Service requests to end the quota system, insisting that the separate white and black calls be maintained. Only much later would it be phased out.

Perhaps the principal reason the Army failed to meet its target was that it did not have adequate training facilities for black soldiers. Segregation was the rule in an Army that had not previously had duplicate facilities. New Army posts had to be built for blacks and new facilities were required on existing posts. In fact, because of the Army's acceptance of Southern standards, segregated facilities had to be introduced on Northern military posts. For example, where whites and blacks had been able to attend movies together (and still could off post), segregated theaters had to be built.

In addition, leadership cadres for new black soldiers were woefully lacking. Only about one-third of one percent of blacks in the Army were officers in 1942. Even when the number of black officers grew, they were seldom assigned to lead black troops nor ever allowed to outrank white officers in the same unit. On some military bases, no separate facilities existed to house or feed them. White officers assigned to command black units were often rejects from white units or Southerners, resented by the troops, especially the troops from the North. This lack of adequate leadership for black units also served to hold down draft calls.

Not only did these policies reduce military efficiency, create unnecessary expense and underutilize the available black personnel, but they also seriously undermined support for the war effort. Perhaps the most egregious blow to morale was the November 1941 revelation that the Red Cross had created segregated blood banks. The Red Cross publicly acknowledged that there was no race-based difference in blood and said that it had been ordered to seg-regate by the Army. The Army Surgeon General admitted that the policy existed because of the opposition of some white soldiers, and it remained in effect throughout the war. Blacks were furious, because Charles R. Drew, a black doc-tor, had developed the plasma process and headed the first Red Cross blood bank.

And, as Hastie pointed out, the Army came nowhere near the objectives of the 1940 Plan embodied in Selective Service. By the end of 1942, four times as high a percentage of enlisted blacks were in service units as compared with combat units.[139] Yet blacks flowed into the Army. Not only did the draft bring its quota numbers, but many blacks vol-untarily enlisted simply because the Army offered them a paycheck, which they could not always obtain in civilian life. On August 31, 1939, 3,640 black soldiers served; on November 30, 1941, there were 97,725.[140] At the end of 1942, there would be 467,883 black troops.[141] But the new soldiers were not assigned to all types of Army units.

At first, many of the black soldiers found themselves assigned to Engineer Separate Battalions.[142] They were clearly "separate" but not equal; these were the infamous labor battalions, the traditional dumping ground of unskilled black soldiers, assigned to do pick-and-shovel work. But the Army needed more than the Separate Battalions could pro-vide, and they were, after all, units smaller than regiments, the smallest units that could be "intermingled" with white units.

The Engineer Separate Battalions began to be expanded and converted into Engineer General Service Regiments, capable of serving as independent units. The work of these units was to build roads and bridges and to operate utilities, requiring a much higher level of skill than those of a laborer.[143] But here, probably because it was faced with an inflow of black troops that had to be assigned somewhere, the War Department forced the Corps of Engineers to accept less skilled workers, presumably either to train them or get rid of them as best it could.

The result was a ready supply, perhaps an oversupply, of so-called "Engineer General Service (Colored) Regiments." Only one such unit had been planned in 1940; by the end of 1942, there would be 27 of them. As a result, some 42 per cent of the Corps of Engineers were black troops by the time work on the Alcan Highway began.[144]

CHAPTER 5.

RACE ON THE ROAD

The Alcan Highway began in March 1942, and the pioneer road, permitting transit to Alaska, was not expected to be completed until sometime in 1943, possibly too late to be of much use in defending Alaska. The use of the three black regiments would make possible the completion of the pioneer road before the end of 1942 and the onset of the depth of winter. The rapid mobilization on the road might be timely enough to contribute to the defense of Alaska.

Blacks leaders had continuously hammered on the need to assign black troops to combat units and not so heavily to support commands. In one of *The American Soldier* surveys, conducted by the Army, 68 percent of blacks believed they were not "getting as much chance as they should to help win the war." Only 20 percent of whites agreed.[145] Alcan would give blacks the opportunity to play a key role, though not in a combat zone.

The use of the three black regiments, however necessary, had to overcome a variety of obstacles. Objections to their use, some coming even as they were deployed, ranged from opposition to assigning them outside of the United States to claims that they would not be able to stand the cold.

Immediately after Pearl Harbor, the Army compiled a list of units ready to service overseas.[146] Eleven black units were on the list, including the three black Engineer regiments sent to the Alcan.

Just how exceptional it was to send black units abroad while Pearl Harbor still echoed is illustrated by what happened in Australia, the other of the two initial overseas posts to which blacks were sent. Despite being fearful of an imminent attack by Japan, Australia had to be convinced by General Douglas MacArthur to accept American black troops, who were immediately sent to help defend it. Later, even some governments of countries with majority black populations but still under colonial rule would object to U.S. black troops, because their role might give rise to unacceptable aspirations among the natives.[147] In part because of such opposition from host counties and partly because of the lower share of black troops in combat units, relatively few black troops served overseas, making those assigned to Alcan unusual. When some officers voiced opposition to sending the three regiments, the need for them drove Secretary Stimson to order Marshall in March 1942 to reject the complaints with this curt message: "No, don't yield."[148]

But racism would be hard to overcome. *The American Soldier* survey showed that 90 percent of whites supported segregation in the Army, while 78 percent of blacks opposed it.[149] The only way that the troops could be assigned to the Alcan, while catering to such views, would be to keep them away from the white units.

Traditional, ingrained reflex racism that had existed in the Army during World War I persisted into the start of the new conflict. Not only were blacks deemed by most officers to be unsuitable for combat service, but many white officers thought they were simply inferior. Coupled with this belief was the concern that the use of blacks, particularly from the South, would only make them "uppity" and more difficult to keep in their place later.

The classic objection came from Brig. Gen. Simon Bolivar Buckner, head of the Alaska Defense Command. He was not just any Southerner; his father had surrendered to Gen. U.S. Grant at Fort Donelson, Tennessee, in the famous exchange in which Grant first demanded unconditional surrender, an order which the senior Buckner thought was both "ungenerous and unchivalrous."[150] The junior Buckner was later to distinguish himself in the war as the highest ranking officer to be killed in combat, when he raised his head out of a foxhole on Okinawa after he had been warned not to do so.

Brig. Gen. Clarence Sturdevant, the Assistant Chief of Engineers, had written him: "I have heard that you object to having colored troops in Alaska and we have attempted to avoid sending them. However, we have been forced to use two colored regiments and it seems unwise for diplomatic reasons to use them both in Canada since the Canadians also prefer whites."[151]

Buckner replied:

> The thing which I have opposed principally has been their establishment as point troops for the unloading of transports at our docks. The very high wages offered to unskilled labor here would attract a large number of them to remain and settle after the war, with the natural result that they would interbreed with the Indians and Eskimos and produce an astonishingly objectionable race of mongrels which would be a problem from now on. We have enough racial problems here and elsewhere. I have no objection whatever to your employing them on the roads if they are kept far enough from the settlements and kept busy and then sent home as soon as possible[152]

Just how these remarks fit within the limits of a normal military communication is difficult to discern. Buckner would clearly have let his personal predilections about race relations influence military decisions, but he was forced to concede that the troops could be used.

Sturdevant's message contained statements that he knew to be untrue, but used to placate Buckner. There were three "colored" regiments already on the way or in place, not two, and two of them would serve in Canada, where no objection had been raised to the use of black troops.[153]

Perhaps the most frequently heard reason for opposing the use of black troops was that they were not as intelligent as whites. One did not have to be a racist; there were simply test scores, which proved scientifically the superior intelligence of whites, the claim went.

Once a man was inducted into the Army, he was given the Army General Classification Test, to determine if he were a fast or slow learner. The AGCT was designed to measure "(1) native capacity, (2) schooling and educational opportunities, (3) socioeconomic status, and (4) cultural background."[154] The Chief Psychologist in the Army's Classification Branch said of the test: "It does not measure merely inherent mental capacity. Performance in such a test reflects very definitely the educational opportunities the individual has had and the way the educational opportunities have been grasped and utilized.... There is nothing in the title of the Army test that says anything about native intelligence."[155] The results of the tests were widely known, and they showed significant differences between whites and blacks. The results for whites generally reflected the bell curve, because the curve had been designed around their scores, so naturally the results for blacks did not.[156]

Table 1. Distribution of Army General Classification Test Scores March 1941-December 1942[157]

AGCT Grade	White	Negro	Total
I	6.6	0.4	6.0
II	28.0	3.4	25.6
III	32.1	12.3	30.2
IV	24.8	34.7	25.7
V	8.5	49.2	12.5
Percentage	90.4	9.6	100.0

The variation of blacks from the designed bell curve suggests what would later be recognized as cultural bias in the test, almost certainly devised by whites. With the two racial groups not further broken down, the test did not actually make a racial comparison using people of similar educational backgrounds and experience. Only in that way might it have been possible to draw distinctions based on race, if there had been any difference in the scores.

The 1940 Census had shown that young males, 18 to 20, had widely different educational backgrounds.[158] In the North, 23% of whites and 34% of blacks had only a grade school education. In the South, 42% of whites and 79% of blacks had only a grade school education. Almost 80 percent of the black male population lived in the South. The test simply failed to take into account these facts: about 80 percent of black males lived in the South and about 80 percent of those of most likely draft age had only completed segregated grade school. *The American Soldier* survey showed that only 39 percent of Southern whites thought that "Negroes can learn as well as whites," compared with 67 percent of whites in the North.[159]

The test was at least suspect, if not invalid, and certainly could not be taken as a measure of intelligence. Nonetheless, it was. Undoubtedly it served as the basis for assigning blacks to manual labor rather than combat and for unit commanders to object to the assignment of blacks to their organizations. Such commanders feared inundation by large groups of "unintelligent" blacks, making it difficult or impossible to train them satisfactorily. Hastie recognized that, with integration, smaller numbers of blacks would be added to any unit, making it more likely they could be trained and not undermine unit efficiency in the process. He was ignored.

A few officers recognized that the AGCT was not a good indicator of performance. "I have come to the fixed opinion that the AGCT is not worth a damn with colored troops,"[160] said one white commander of black troops. The solution for overcoming the lack of apparent ability of blacks (and whites) scoring low on a test that had not been devised with them in mind was obvious — more and better training. And commanders were advised, mostly in vain, to recognize other factors: "There are many other qualities which must be taken into consideration such as perseverance, honesty, physical stamina and loyalty and loyalty is not the least of these,"[161] one commander told a training conference. Presumably, these factors applied to the three black Engineer General Service Regiments that were deemed ready for duty on the Alcan Highway.

But training could not always overcome prejudice. When the black 95th Engineers arrived at Dawson Creek, B.C., in late May 1942, it found it had been stripped of its heavy equipment and relegated to road finishing work behind the white 341st, already on the ground. While the white unit had a month's experience on the road, it was a newly formed and poorly trained unit, while the 95th had both extensive training and experience. Col. James A. "Patsy" O'Connor, in charge of the construction on the southern portion of the road, defied the textbook approach of assigning the more experienced unit, and put the black troops in a support role. Undoubtedly, O'Connor, who had never dealt with black troops, was influenced by "some extremely derogatory ideas about blacks that were prevalent in the command hierarchy of the U.S. Army."[162] O'Connor gave some signs later of changing his mind, and the 95th got better road-building assignments.

Black enlisted personnel could find it difficult to break out of this stereotype. General Davis spent some of his time identifying soldiers for Officer Candidate School. But many found that administrative obstacles prevented them from demonstrating their ability to learn and to lead. One soldier in the 97th Regiment reported that he had been selected for OCS, but was told that he had lost his eligibility simply because his unit moved.[163]

As if being considered inferior and unintelligent was not enough, blacks would not be able to stand the cold, according to military doctrine. This was a racial stereotype, and it clearly was an excuse for racist officers to attempt to exclude blacks. The road would be built in the coldest corner of North America, at least where temperatures are recorded, where the record low of 81.4 degrees below zero would be set in the Yukon near the Alaska border.[164]

In fact, the Army had developed a policy against sending black troops to extreme northern climates without any scientific basis. The war would reveal only anecdotal evidence that blacks, notably those from the South, reacted differently from whites to the cold. For example, in a truck convoy from Nebraska to Kansas, 18 serious cases of frozen feet affected the black drivers, but only one of the 30 white drivers was similarly affected. Most of the blacks were from Arkansas, Louisiana and Texas. Some suggested that such cases might be caused by chronic deficiency diseases. Whatever the reason, the Army considered such instances as supporting the notion that blacks could not stand the cold as well as whites.[165]

The fact that racism more than science was at work was evidenced by objections not only to blacks being assigned to cold areas, but also to warm locations, including Panama. Stimson had rejected both cold and hot disqualifications, saying about Panama: "it is ridiculous to raise such objections when the Panama Canal itself was built by black labor."[166] Actually, American blacks had not been used because they were not considered strong enough to work in the heat, an indication that stereotyping by climate was nothing new.[167]

After the war, the Army Surgeon General reported that: [i]n World War II, observations...furnished no indications that United States Negroes or other soldiers native to Southern States were any more or less susceptible to cold injuries than were other troops. Combat comparisons are not valid because a large proportion of Negro troops were assigned to service organizations and did not suffer much exposure."[168]

The Surgeon General might have looked at the Alcan experience, where white and black support troops worked under similar conditions. No evidence exists to show that blacks suffered any more from the cold than did the white troops on the Alcan, when they were similarly equipped.

Col. Walter F. von Zelinski, the chief medical officer of the Northwest Service Command, the umbrella unit for the Alcan Highway and related projects, said that out of the more than 20,000 men involved in all projects, only 140 were incapacitated by the cold and all but four recovered completely. The four had one or two toes amputated. "In my opinion," he said, "this constitutes an all-time record for protection of the human body in the coldest imaginable temperatures."[169]

This conclusion explains what happened: one would never get the chance to know if either race were more susceptible to the cold, if everybody bundled up. The troops knew they had to take precautions. As the cold weather set in, they jettisoned the leather boots they had been provided and even the shoepaks, which had rubber bottoms. Instead, they used canvas galoshes. Similarly, they replaced heavy woolen socks with layers of lighter socks. A white officer later reported that he had been asked frequently "how my black Southern soldiers got along in the subfreezing arctic weather. On one occasion when the temperature fell to 72 degrees below zero for one three-week period, they got along as well as anyone else."[170] They kept covered and used the buddy system.

After the initial road building was completed and, during the winter of 1942-43, when the units were assigned maintenance and improvement, an inspector visited the 97th, the black regiment in interior Alaska. The temperature was at 63 below, and he found the unit "pathetically ill-equipped [and] doing little else but hibernating at present.... As a result of worn out clothing and lack of essential equipment, their outdoor working capacity has been reduced to a small fraction of summer efficiency...."[171] This unit had come from Florida with summer equipment and had only been gradually outfitted for the cold climate.

Not only was frostbite seldom encountered, but any form of cold injury or illness was rare. One black soldier died when he tried to walk from his stalled vehicle back to base. Knowledge of this story was so widespread that it served as a warning to all the other troops. There was virtually no incidence of respiratory diseases because, it was supposed, the black troops were kept in virtual isolation from others.[172] The 1942-43 Annual Medical report of the Northwest Service Command found that only 1.82 percent of personnel had reported for sick call, concluding that the "remarkably low rate for all diseases was astonishing."[173] In fact, the only relevant medical finding was that about four-fifths of the troops suffered from runny noses.

The only cold-related handicap suffered by black and white soldiers, almost without distinction, was the lack of proper cold weather gear. Civilian contractors, working for the Public Roads Administration during that same winter to begin the upgrade of the road, were properly equipped and, by contrast, were not pinned down by the cold.

Finally, the black troops had to overcome widespread beliefs about their character. The most frequently used cliché was that they were "lazy and shiftless." The cliche itself was embodied in a motion picture actor known as Steppin Fetchit, who was shown as slow, venal and subservient.[174] In fact, the character was far from the reality of black performance, but in deciding where to assign blacks, where to send units and what work to give them, Steppin Fetchit-like characteristics were often attached to all blacks.

There appears to have been a reason for these characteristics being associated with at least some blacks, but nobody bothered to investigate. In the post-Civil War period, poverty swept the South and with it came the spread of disease. Although not fully recognized until the next century, malaria, hookworm and pellagra had become widespread in the South but were almost nonexistent elsewhere. Together, these maladies were known as "diseases of laziness," because they "sapped the strength" of their victims.[175] In fact, these diseases contributed to Southerners being different, "native foreigners" in their own country.[176] These maladies hit the poor, both black and white, but because most Southern blacks were poor, the "diseases of laziness" affected them much more and supported the Steppin Fetchit image. By the start of the war, these diseases had largely been brought under control, but the image lingered.

The cumulative effect of the pressures on black troops caused morale to be lower among them than among white troops. *The American Soldier* surveys showed, for example, that among troops in the Aleutians, the "morale of Negro troops is low."[177] A survey elsewhere in the Pacific area, showed that 41 percent of black and only 19 percent of whites said: "I am usually low in spirits."[178]

The black Engineer units were even more isolated than the white regiments, whose soldiers sometimes visited the small towns along the road. Blacks were not allowed in native villages, and they did not have facilities to duplicate some of the services available to whites in town. One reported: "We were not allowed in the Service Clubs that white troops went in and there were no Service Clubs for blacks."[179] A survey showed that 46 percent of white Southern soldiers and 22 percent of those from the North thought that blacks "should find recreation facilities of their own" and not use the same buildings as whites.[180] So the hard work in the bush was not the only reason for feeling isolated. Despite repeated efforts by the Army to improve leisure opportunities for blacks, unit commanders continued to ban blacks from white recreation facilities until the end of the war. For recreation, the black troops had to rely on themselves. Said one Canadian who worked on the road: "I mean the niggers. They didn't know anything. They'd sit around and one would say something, a mumble and the rest would laugh. You never knew what they said. Like it was their own language. Nice guys though."[181]

The 97th Engineers, the only Army unit, black or white, assigned to road construction in Alaska itself, worked in an area far from any town and its black troops were barred from any contact with native settlements. Gen. Buckner's conditions had been met. From the depths of their isolation, some troops actually wondered if they would ever get home.

This physical isolation was aggravated by the Army's efforts to keep them from getting news from home. As part of a general policy, rescinded later by a direct order from President Roosevelt, black newspapers were not allowed on Army posts nor would mail subscriptions be delivered to soldiers on the Alcan. In February 1942, whites in Detroit had resisted the placement of black workers in the Sojourner Truth development, which had been built to house factory labor moving in from the South. News of the resulting riot and its aftermath, as well as other domestic racial unrest, was to be kept from the black troops. The black press was also running the Double V campaign, and soldiers were to be shielded from that as well. The effort failed, because the Army did not censor incoming letters from home, containing clippings on the riots.

On rare occasions, black troops did visit civilian settlements. Often the results there were discouraging. Reporting on Fairbanks, an Alaska Department Intelligence officer said: "Some stores have reported that the Negroes so far have been well behaved, but it is thought that this attitude would be short lived."[182] The next week he reported: "Local law enforcement agencies report that the conduct of the negro soldier while in Fairbanks had been equally good, if not superior, as that of the white soldier." But people were signing a petition saying the black soldiers should be used in places "more closely resembling their natural habitat."[183]

In B.C. and the Yukon, Canadians saw American blacks in large numbers for the first time. "Cotton-pickers before they joined up or were conscripted, small farm boys, boys from the slums of the big cities," one observed. "They were nothing, just labor battalions." He continued: "In those days they were segregated and they did all the rough work. Some drove trucks and machines, tractors, but they also did an awful lot of pure backbreaking bull labor, axe work and pick and shovel. And they hated it.... They were segregated in a land of nowhere and they were miserable."[184]

Another Canadian, a released convict on his way to work on the road, commented: "The Negro fellows were the work battalions and I thought they were like slaves. Everybody kicked them around...."[185] This was one man's introduction to U.S. official racism.

The success of black units and the morale of the troops depended heavily on the quality of leadership. The Engineer units had white officers, as did most black Army units. The only black officers in the three regiments on the Alcan were chaplains, not command personnel. But chaplains were themselves subject to discrimination. Except for Edward Carroll, a black chaplain with Ivy League credentials who one day would be a Methodist bishop, the chaplains could not take their meals with the white officers and ate alone.

In 1942, "a special inspector reported to the War Department that there was a tendency to assign white officers of mediocre caliber to Negro units and that leadership in many units was therefore deficient."[186] When sent to black units, new junior officers frequently felt that they were getting second-rate assignments, because they were being penalized for not doing better in training.[187]

It was also widely believed by both whites and blacks that Southern-bred officers were assigned disproportionately to black units, because they "understood" blacks better than Northerners, based on their long experience with them. One Southern soldier, who clearly preferred Northern officers, found his regimental leaders "hard guys."[188] One white officer wrote home about some of his fellows: "Strange as it seems, these dastardly punks are Southerners. The Army works for them, and the colored man is still his slave. I'd like to line them up against a stone wall and then convert them to fertilizer."[189]

Southern soldiers may have "understood" those officers and not been shocked by their treatment and the epithets applied to some of them, while they may have been more uncertain about their treatment by Northerners, who ranged from being sympathetic to being racist. Northern blacks, almost a third of the black soldiers, were less happy with such leadership. One soldier wrote: "That old Southern principle of keeping Negroes as slaves is still being practiced." Another recounted that his captain "told a boy if he didn't be quite [sic], he make him. The boy told him that the first time he tryed [sic] to close his mouth he would cut his throat. The boy really meant it."[190] Anecdotal evidence suggests that, in some cases including the three Alcan regiments, the Army assigned some Northern, Jewish officers, presumably assumed to be less biased.

Where white officers demonstrated good leadership skills, especially in convincing black soldiers that they were being treated fairly at least within the unit, they led successful units. A major factor in successful leadership was the direct and sympathetic interest shown by white officers in the black troops. One company officer later wrote a book about his experiences in Company C of the 93rd Battalion (soon to be a regiment), one of the black units on the Alcan. He recounted the need to provide education in simple matters of personal hygiene and a sense of military discipline, with which the troops were unfamiliar. Some of these troops, mostly from the South, were illiterate and were taught how to sign their name. They responded well to this command attention, probably because no white person had ever taken such close and committed interest in them. Such additional work imposed a greater burden on the officers than those commanding white units, and, contrary to the original policy, no additional officers were assigned to black units than to white ones.

The white officers in the 93rd recognized that they needed better educated recruits to serve as noncommissioned officers. At their request, the War Department allowed the battalion to send out a team to recruit 36 men at Tugaloo College in Mississippi and Grambling College in Louisiana to serve as non-commissioned officers. At least one of these recruits became a major in a black infantry division by the end of the war. As better educated Northern blacks joined the unit, they took on leadership roles.[191]

Despite low morale, discipline did not pose a problem. When the 93rd Regiment had been delayed at Skagway, one case of rape by a black soldier occurred there. This single act fed the stereotype of black social behavior. But, after the Engineers' work was done, the Northwest Service Command reported only six additional charges of unlawful sexual contact, four by blacks and two by whites. No black was charged with rape; one black was charged with "attempt to kiss."[192] This low crime rate was probably one positive result of isolation.

The almost complete absence of disciplinary problems did not indicate acquiescence or passivity. Beneath the surface, resentment was growing. Troops of the 95th Regiment, which had suffered the most obvious discrimination on the Alcan Highway, were reassigned from Canada to Camp Alexander, Louisiana, where they were hassled by the local police. While there, they were denied the use of knives at meals and were allowed only to use spoons when they ate. They were next assigned to Camp Shanks, N.Y., the port of embarkation for Europe. Their resentment finally boiled over; they threatened to kill their Southern officers, and a riot broke out. The troops were confined to quarters and quickly shipped out. One of the soldiers recalled that "the Southern-born [blacks] were used to the treatment, but the Northerners wouldn't take no more than they had to."[193]

This event was not unusual. The authoritative Army study of race relations reported that "the Army's files are replete with cases of discrimination charged, investigations launched, and exonerations issued or reforms ordered. An incredible amount of time and effort went into handling these cases during the darkest days of the war – cases growing out of a policy created in name of military efficiency."[194] In the Army study of black troops' participation in the war, the section on racial disturbances, too numerous to document, was called "Harvest of Disorder."[195]

The most important judgment about the black troops must be whether they did the job they had been sent to do. Even after the fact, controversy remained.

The task of the seven Engineer regiments was to build a pioneer or tote road, not a finished highway. The goal was to build a road that would be passable enough to truck supplies to Alaska and the Northwest Staging Route until an all-weather road could be built. Because Alaska seemed vulnerable, speed was essential, and for that reason, the three black regiments had been sent to work with the white units.

The road was completed in a single construction season, because of the work done by all seven regiments; no officer then or later would claim that the pioneer road could have been completed before sometime in 1943 without the involvement of a force larger than the original four regiments.

The road's progress is best illustrated by a table developed by a congressional committee:

Table 2. Mileage Under Construction[196]

To date indicated	Mileage	Remarks
Apr. 30	8	By Thirty-fifth Engineers
May 31	95	By 4 regiments
June 30	360	By 7 regiments
July 31	794	"
Aug. 31	*1186	Fort Nelson reached Aug. 26
Sept. 30	*1479	Road passable to Whitehorse, Sept. 24
Oct. 25	*1645	Road passable to Fairbanks

*Includes Public Roads Administration construction.

The bare numbers provide the basic answer. Perhaps the leading historian of the road has concluded that the black troops did "remarkably well," although "their efficiency and proficiency were somewhat less as a whole than the white regiments,"[197] which had tougher assignments. But he also wrote that the commander's "low opinion of their reliability and technical competence is revealed by the failsafe missions he gave them."[198]

Given the way the road was built, one unit following another with the Public Roads Administration hard on their heels upgrading the pioneer road as soon as the Engineers moved on, it was difficult to attribute some of the formidable accomplishment to specific units. As Twichell, the road's historian, concluded, the credit for the black unit's contributions by white officers "was colored by their perceptions of blacks at the time."[199]

Nothing illustrates the issue of the black contribution better than Twichell's story of an initiative taken by his own father, then commanding the 95th Engineers, the unit that had been stripped of its heavy equipment. In fact, the Alcan Highway commanders could only give primary road-building responsibilities to two black regiments, because only two could be kept reasonably isolated.[200] The 95th had been relegated to upgrading the road built by the 341st. Twichell volunteered his regiment to build the bridge over the Sikanni Chief River. His offer was accepted, as that would allow the 341st to move ahead more rapidly with road clearing. But the bridge had to be completed within a week.

The river was 300 feet across and flowed rapidly through a wooded gorge, and the crossing would be difficult. Armed only with hand tools, axes and sledge hammers, the troops built a solid structure, able to withstand ice flows that would destroy many of the other bridges on the pioneer road. The bridge was completed in 72 hours, less than half the time allotted. The 95th's commander thought the bridge had cured the regiment's morale problems, perhaps misinterpreting a momentary sense of accomplishment for the kind of change that would only be achieved if they got their equipment back, which never happened. Still, higher command was pleased and had the 95th build bridges for the 341st, instead of simply trailing along behind it.[201]

As the memory of the Alcan Highway has faded, so has the role of the black troops. Some writers have created the inaccurate belief that the blacks had not received credit for their part in its construction.[202] Army historians, seeking to be both complete and objective if not writers of popular literature, noted their contribution. Word spread in the black community.

The final link of the pioneer road had been closed on October 25, 1942, by the meeting of two Caterpillar earth movers, one from the black 97th from the North and the other from the white 18th. When they met near Beaver Creek, Yukon, Corporal Refines Sims, Jr., of Philadelphia and the 97th, shook hands with Private Alfred Jafulka of

Kennedy, Texas and the 18th. The leading historian of black participation in World War II wrote that "the meeting between white and Negro drivers symbolized to a hopeful country the kind of unity and cooperation that foretold eventual victory. Public speakers and radio programs made much of the symbolism of the event for months to come."[203] The attention seems mainly to have been among blacks.

Norman Rosten had written a poem, *The Big Road*, heard on the radio networks and then published in a book. He imagined the meeting between Jafulka and Sims:

> Dismount, pause,
> Stumble forward, alive, black man and white man,
> "Where you been soldier?"
>   "Lookin' for you, soldier!"
> "You been lost?"
>   "Maybe – didn't have time to ask."
> "I been lookin' for you so long my eyes hurt!"
> "Rough road. Plenty rough. Whole idea crazy as hell
> But we did it I guess. Got it goin' somewhere."
> "Seems like it's goin' clean around the world,
> Won't never stop. Cold, eh?"
>   "Cigarette, corporal?
> "Corporal Sims, Jr., hail from Philadelphia."
> "Private First Class Jafulka, state of Texas.
> Pleased to meet you."
>   The match flickers
> Between their cupped hands. They inhale deeply.[204]

At the closing ceremonies, on November 20, 1942 at a place christened Soldier's Summit, "Patsy" O'Connor, now a general, went out of his way to praise the black troops. Four soldiers held the ribbon for the inevitable symbolic opening. In addition to Sims and Jafulka, a black and a white soldier from the southern sector of the road had been selected.

At a time when unrest was growing among black Americans, both inside and outside of the military, the ceremony and the road itself contributed to the massive effort of the U.S. government to increase the commitment of all Americans to the war effort. What had started out as the use of black troops because of military necessity had turned out to combat exploits of the Tuskegee airmen and others that were still well in the future, the Alcan experience was the major propaganda coup in the struggle for black support.

But propaganda should never be confused with reality. The 95th had never had its own equipment nor its own segment of the road, mostly because of the racial antipathy of the white commanders. Instead of complaining that black troops had not received enough credit for their work, commentators might have focused on the failure to give them the work.

Despite the actual achievements of the black units and the media splash made of their participation, segregation would continue. The attitudes of the white commanders, still steeped in World War I lore and the Southern experience, never changed.

General Hoge, the first commander of the Alcan Highway forces, was not at the Soldier's Summit ceremonies. He had moved on from the Engineers to become an Armored commander in Europe and retired in 1955 as a four-star general and Commander-in-Chief, U.S. Army Europe. Interviewed by the Army in 1974, 32 years after the road and almost a decade after the revolution of the Voting Rights Act, Hoge, a Southerner, spoke of the black Engineers:

> They could do pick and shovel work and that was about all. I remember up there when we got that regiment [the 97th]...in at Valdez. Those niggers just looked at all that snow — it was all white...they had to go across the mountains up through that pass and get over into the valley beyond....They got worried about whether they were going to get out of there and...I told them...the only way you're going to get home — back to Alabama or Georgia — is to work down south. Head south and keep working ... because they took all the ships out behind them. [The 97th] were just left there. They were practically useless.[205]

Thanks for your help, Corporal Sims.

Part III. "The Greatest Achievement Since the Panama Canal"

Alcan Projects

ALASKA

AKLAVIK

FAIRBANKS McPHERSON ARCTIC RED RIVER

DISTRICT OF MACKENZIE

GOOD HOPE

YUKON CANOL CAMP NORMAN WELLS

WRIGLEY

WHITEHORSE

TESLIN SIMPSON

SKAGWAY PROVIDENCE

WATSON LAKE

HAY RIVER

BRITISH FORT NELSON FT. SMITH
COLUMBIA CHIPEWYAN
EMBARRAS

FORT ST. JOHN

PRINCE RUPERT

DAWSON CREEK WATERWAYS McMURRAY

GRANDE
PRINCE GEORGE PRAIRIE

EDMONTON

ALBERTA

| 0 | 100 | 200 | 300 | 400 |

SCALE IN MILES

MACKENZIE RIVER WATER ROUTE
PIPELINE
PIPELINE ALONG HIGHWAY
ALASKA MILITARY HIGHWAY
AIR ROUTE

Source: NAC, RG 36/7, vol. 14, file 22-23 from Grant, *Sovereignty or Security?*

CHAPTER 6.

THE ROAD NORTH

The War Department's order to Col. Hoge, assigning him the task of finding the route and organizing the troops, was that the road "will be pushed to completion within the physical capacity of the troops."[206] Hoge would soon be promoted to Brigadier General, he would be given the troops required, and his force would be organized into a provisional brigade. He knew that the Alcan Highway had to be built quickly or there would be no point building it at all.

The plan, as ordered by the War Department in February was simple to state and difficult to do:

> It is desired that you undertake the construction, with Engineer troops, of a pioneer-type road from Fort St. John, Canada, to Big Delta, Alaska, via Fort Nelson, Canada, Watson Lake, Canada, Whitehorse, Canada, and Boundary, Alaska. It is further desired that you arrange with the Public Roads Administration to follow the Engineer troops, to correct alignment and grade, construct permanent bridges and culverts, and provide for the completion of the project.[207]

What neither those giving the orders nor those receiving them knew were the route to follow, how to construct a road in the wilderness with unskilled personnel, how to deal with the problems of muskeg and permafrost, how many troops would be available, and when they would arrive, how long the building season would last and the deadline for completing the road. The only point that was evident to Hoge from the start was that he would begin receiving Engineer troops almost immediately, well before the PRA contractors would arrive to do the follow-up work.

Even as the first regiment was arriving at Dawson Creek, Hoge realized that four regiments would be insufficient and that other entry points would have to be found. In response to his request, the Army added the three "colored" regiments. Hoge decided that each regiment would be assigned a stretch of the road to build.[208]

According to the plan, the pioneer road known as the Alcan Highway would be built by Engineer troops, and the PRA would turn this primitive road into a wider, all-weather road after the Engineers had completed their work.

The first two units to arrive were Combat Engineer Regiments. By April 11, they had begun building the Alcan Highway. But route selection would reveal a major interagency conflict and threaten to slow progress. The Corps of Engineers had been assigned to bring the PRA into the project. The PRA engineers would not go along with the Engineers' route determinations, and the PRA itself would not take orders from Brig. Gen. Clarence L. Sturdevant, Assistant to the Chief of Engineers and the Corps officer in charge of the Alcan Highway. In effect, two different groups were vying for the power to decide where the road would be built. Here was a classic turf battle — over turf.

Gen. Sturdevant finally came to terms with the PRA. In other words, he surrendered. Sturdevant agreed to changes in the planned route without informing Hoge. Even more importantly, he had assigned responsibility for building segments of the pioneer road directly to the PRA, taking the authority away from Hoge. Hoge received the word from the local PRA chief, and he was furious, causing a rift to develop between him and Sturdevant. The war over route location and road quality between the Engineers, instructed to build a simple, one-lane dirt road, and the PRA, already planning the wider, all-weather road, continued for months.[209]

By May, Hoge's position as field commander had further deteriorated, and his decline was not merely a

personnel matter. It reflected the increasing domination of
the project by one of the top people in the Army, Lt. Gen.
Brehon B. Somervell, the chief of the Services of Supply,
which included the Corps of Engineers. The Army had been
divided into three parts, the ground forces, the Air Corps
and Somervell's services, which provided support for the
other two parts. As a result, Somervell had immense power
and reported directly to Marshall.

In August, Somervell came to the Yukon. The road
seemed certain to be completed in a single year instead of
two. Still, Hoge clashed with Somervell. When Somervell
got back to Washington, he decided "Hoge has to go."[210]

Hoge's removal was actually part of a bigger plan. The
Northwest Service Command was created, directly under
Somervell, whose control of his "empire" was now complete and direct. Somewhat mysteriously, Sturdevant found
himself reassigned with no further responsibility for the
Alcan Highway.[211] Somervell had no possible second-
guesser left in the War Department.

Summer ends in the deep Northwest around September
1, and the completion of the road took place with the onset
of one of the area's harshest winters, with temperatures
reportedly as low as 70 below. Hoge had expected that the
road was to be built in two seasons and that the troops
would be sent back to the United States until they could
resume work again in 1943. As a result, they were ill-pre-
pared to keep working into the winter, having little winter
clothing and housed in canvas tents. While supplies gradually filtered in to some units, most were forced to keep fires
burning continuously, so that troops could warm themselves
while they worked. Even after the opening ceremonies in
November 1942, the troops stayed on through the heart of
the winter to maintain what they had built. Soldiers, none of
whom was sent home for a winter with a record low of
minus 71, were bitter. Winter deserves a share of the credit
for the road being passable before the end of 1942. Frozen
ground and rivers made passage easier.

At times it may have seemed as if the road building was taking place in complete isolation from the rest of the war. The ability of the Engineers and PRA to get the pioneer road open in 1942 instead of the following year as originally planned, was more a result of their having come to grips with the complexities of sub-arctic construction and one another and their desire to leave the inhospitable North as soon as possible rather than of an enhanced sense of urgency. Yet there was a war going on, and it looked like some of the threats to Alaska might be realized.

Somewhat to its surprise, Japan had found itself vulnerable when Doolittle raided Tokyo. Though the Pearl Harbor attack had failed to destroy American aircraft carriers, at sea at the time, there was speculation in Japan whether the B-25s had come from Alaska and not their actual launching point on the *U.S.S. Hornet.* The naval plan developed after the Doolittle raid was intended to allow the Japanese to deal with both aircraft carriers and Alaska.

In early May 1942, the Japanese fleet was ordered to attack Midway Island in hopes of drawing American aircraft carriers into a battle where they would be at last destroyed. At the same time, a force composed of two aircraft carriers, two heavy cruisers and three destroyers would destroy the American base at Dutch Harbor, Alaska, and occupy three other Aleutian Islands – Attu, Kiska and Adak.[212]

The prime reason for the attack on the Aleutians was to draw American forces away from Midway, the focal point of the campaign. The Japanese also sought to establish bases from which they could bomb Alaska and the United States. Finally, they hoped to disrupt the northern link between the United States and the Soviet Union.

The United States had broken the Japanese Naval code and understood the plan. On June 3, 1942, the Japanese began their bombing attacks on Dutch Harbor, having relatively little effect and not drawing the attention of the main U.S. Pacific fleet. The next day, the battle of Midway was under way, and, as the situation deteriorated for them, the

Japanese tried to recall their northern elements. The brief battle of Dutch Harbor, which caused screaming headlines in the United States, brought another Japanese setback when it yielded one of the major intelligence breaks of the Pacific war, the capture intact of a highly maneuverable Japanese Zero fighter plane. U.S. warplanes could be designed to counter its strengths.

After their stunning defeat at Midway, the Japanese decided to continue with the planned invasion of the Aleutians, mainly to bolster morale at home. On June 7, the Japanese, with vastly superior forces, came ashore at both Kiska and Attu. In fact, the only U.S. military presence on either island consisted of 12 sailors operating a weather station on Kiska. Communications were cut, and the Alaska command assumed that the islands had been occupied, which could only be confirmed by an overflight three days later. Weather had covered the get-away of the Japanese northern fleet.

The occupation of Attu and Kiska, among the most remote pieces of American territory, might have been expected to cause alarm in Alaska and act as a spur to road building. However, just as the Americans would take almost a year to get ready to move against the occupiers, they also learned from the observations of the enemy that the Japanese were in no position to launch any attack further to the East. This intelligence came too late to affect the completion of the pioneer road.

The Americans finally attacked Attu in May 1943 and defeated the 2,600 Japanese occupiers, most of whom committed suicide. In August 1943, when they attacked Kiska, which they assumed to be a far more difficult objective, they found that 5,300 enemy troops had been taken off the island by the Japanese Navy, under cover of dense fog. The war in Alaska was over, and the road was just about completed.

When the accounts were tallied, the road project turned out to be extremely costly. The government fixed the cost of the pioneer road at $19,744,585 (2004 Consumer Price

Index = $229,037,186). The cost included charges made by PRA contractors who had deployed 7,500 men in addition to the Engineers, and the civilians had accounted for more than half of the pioneer road expenditures. But the seeming precision of this amount was somewhat illusory as it did not include the cost of paying and supporting the 10,000 troops nor of the 30,568 pieces of major equipment they used. The troops' pay, support and personal equipment alone could easily have accounted for an additional $12,000,000 (2004 = $139,200,000).

The final road cost under PRA supervision, in addition to amounts spent to build the pioneer road, was set at $94,079,635 ($1,091,323,766). At its peak effort, the PRA had used 14,100 men. The cost of the Haines lateral road, including the Engineer's pioneer road, was $12,216,000 ($141,589,600).

By October 1943, the effort had produced an all-weather road from Dawson Creek to Fairbanks at a total cost of more than $138 million ($1.6 billion). But the war in Alaska was over, and, although there was a rail line to Dawson Creek, the Canadians had not built an all-weather road from Edmonton to Dawson Creek. Apparently, nobody had thought to ask them to build it.

To put Alcan Highway expenditures in perspective, the costs represented less than four-tenths of one percent of federal spending in 1942. If the same share of 2002 spending were allocated to such a project, its cost would be about $8 billion, an amount still capable of attracting political attention, but less than a quarter of the initial emergency spending measures taken after the 9/11 attacks.

Two financial aspects of the project drove up its cost. First, there was an enormous amount of waste and theft.

Even more serious in terms of its impact on total cost was the method used for paying the PRA contractors. Because of the remote location of the route, contractors could not study it before they bid nor did they know how much equipment and personnel they would need for the unfamiliar conditions. The PRA decided to use the cost-plus-a-fixed-fee contract that had been approved by Congress. Under this arrangement, the contractor would recover all of its costs and a 5 percent fee. Presumably the government would someday audit the actual costs, and the fee seemed like a reasonable profit margin, although it provided an incentive to boost the costs as much as possible.

There was one approved way to increase costs, and it was a bonanza to the contractors. The PRA paid rent on the contractors' equipment, valued at $15.5 million. During a 17-month period, the rent amounted to $6.5 million, 42 percent of the value of the equipment or an annual return of 29 percent. Virtually all of the equipment was reusable and carted away by the contractors. If the equipment had an actual life of 10 years, for example, the exorbitant rental fees increased the contractors' profit margin by 80 percent.

Nature and the remote location, not subject to anybody's control, served to increase the cost of the project over what roads in the United States would have cost. But the cost-plus payment and rental methods used throughout the war certainly made it a good and profitable business.

When the Alcan Highway pioneer road was completed, it was widely hailed as an engineering achievement comparable to the construction of the Panama Canal, a project which had taken a decade for the Engineers to build. A widely read *National Geographic* article called it "the greatest achievement of the U.S. Corps of Engineers since the construction of the Panama Canal."[213] In 2002 dollars, the Canal cost the United States $6.6 billion, while the Alcan Highway cost $1.6 billion, not even a quarter as much.

A 1943 history of the road by the Northwest Service Command issued what is perhaps the most accurate verdict:

> Many articles have appeared in the newspapers and magazines all over the country describing the Alcan Highway project. In most of these, the writers having been caught with the spirit of the accomplishment, and of the vastness of the country, have described the project as a "miracle of engineering skill" and "a feat comparable to the construction of the Panama Canal." To anyone familiar with the

personnel engaged on the job, and the conditions under which they worked, and with the mission itself, it as apparent that these descriptions are merely flowery exaggerations. The Highway project was not a miracle, nor was any great engineering skill needed for its accomplishment; it was, however, one of the outstanding demonstrations of the fortitude, perseverance, and indomitable spirit of the American soldier.[214]

The road had met the standard of "do something, anything," imposed in the wake of Pearl Harbor. Less than a year after that attack, the Army could send supplies to Alaska over a 1,600-mile, primitive road cut through what had been only recently trackless wilderness.

The speed and sacrifice were impressive, and grist for the American propaganda effort. "To say that it was a faultless performance where no errors of judgment or management took place would not be a supportable statement...," the Congressional Roads Committee concluded, but the road "furnishes us with an example of what American ingenuity and managerial brains can do when confronted with an emergency problem...for which there is no precedent...."[215] The Committee did not investigate to see if the road was worth the effort or served its original purpose.

Eventually, the name Alcan Highway, applied to the pioneer road, faded. In 1943, it became the Alaska Highway, pointing to its future as a civilian highway. As promised, six months after the war ended, the highway was turned over to the Canadians. Yet the Americans lingered on. Because the link from Haines through Canada to the Alaska border provided major land access to Alaska, as important as the highway from the south, the United States undertook to underwrite the ongoing cost of the so-called Shakwak project for improving the Haines cut-off and the Alaska Highway to the border. The actual road building is done by Canadians, and the joint road project lived on into the 21st Century.

CHAPTER 7.

THE SECRET SUCCESS STORY

The only World War II Alcan project initiated by the Canadians was actually first envisaged by an American, Gen. Billy Mitchell, the Army maverick who was probably the most creative military thinker the United States had seen. His concepts included strategic bombing, paratroop attacks behind enemy lines, tactical fighter air support of ground troops and a separate air force. He predicted a Japanese surprise attack and forecast the role Alaska could play in the inevitable response to such an attack. His advocacy, what would later be called "thinking outside the box," was squelched by the Army, and he was ultimately court-martialed for refusing to back down.[216] He would later be proved correct about virtually all of his major proposals, and he was right about Alaska.

On July 15, 1920, four single engine planes took off from Mitchel Field, Long Island, on a 4,500 mile trip to Nome, Alaska.[217] Gen. Mitchell had organized the flight to demonstrate that military planes could fly great distances and the importance of Alaska as an access point to Asia. Four years later, he sent planes around the world, once again using the Alaska route, which greatly reduced the amount of time over open water. In 1934, Lt. Col. H.H. Arnold, who would head the Army Air Corps in World War II, took bombers to Alaska to determine future military needs there, but could not attract congressional funding for even a single air base in Alaska. In 1937, the Soviets showed the merits of the polar, great circle route with three flights to Alaska. Celebrities, including Charles and Anne Morrow

Lindbergh, Wiley Post, and Howard Hughes, flew the route, but interest in the United States remained low.[218]

In 1939, the Canadian Department of Transport began engineering work for airfields at Grande Prairie in Alberta, Fort St. John, Fort Nelson, Watson Lake and Whitehorse.[219] Ottawa was increasingly aware of the need to prepare for war with Japan and had decided that these airfields could contribute to Canada's defense.

The PJBD began its meetings in August 1940 and within two weeks it began to consider the need for military airfields in western Canada. By October, in a report to the two governments, it recommended that Canada should build the airfields as soon as possible. On November 14, 1940, the PJBD formally recommended that "suitable landing fields, complete with emergency lighting, radio aids, meteorological equipment and limited housing for weather, communication, and transient personnel be provided at the earliest possible date by Canada...."[220] In addition to the five already under study, the PJBD added two further to the West.

The recommendation envisaged the use of the airfields "for the rapid movement of light bombers and fighter aircraft" into Canada and Alaska. This action, the recommendation stated, "is considered essential to the defense of Western Canada, Alaska and the United States," showing that 13 months before the attack on Pearl Harbor, the United States and Canada were fully aware that they must be prepared to defend their national territories against a Japanese attack. Because the recommendation dealt only with facilities in Canada, there seemed to be no question that, while the planes would be American, Canada would foot the bill. In addition, it was politically impossible for the still-neutral United States to allocate funds for military construction outside of U.S. territory. The Canadian Government released funds for the airfields in December 1940.

The Canadians called the airway the Northwest Staging Route or NWSR, while the Americans labeled it the Northwest Ferry Route. Whatever it was called, it was not ready for full use when the Japanese attacked on December 7.

Despite the recommendations made the previous year and the agreement of both countries on the need for the airway, neither had unleashed the funds required to respond to the urgency found by the PJBD. The process had revealed that preparedness depended on more than foresight; it required action. Yet the recommendations had served a purpose, because planes could begin limited use of the airway to defend Alaska soon after America entered the war.

The Air Corps immediately assigned a squadron of 25 P-40 fighters and a squadron of 13 B-26 bombers to move to Alaska. None of the crews was trained for flying in Alaska, and the facilities on the NWSR were barely sufficient. Their flight to Alaska was a catastrophe, revealing inadequate preparation and a failure to understand the challenges of winter flying in the Yukon. Gen. Arnold, apparently remembering his own 1935 flight to Alaska, had not appreciated the difficulties.

Three of the bombers became lost on their flight to Watson Lake, and the pilots ditched their planes in deep snow before running completely out of fuel. When the airmen were discovered, huddled in the lead plane, a bush pilot brought in supplies and a Mountie, who could help them survive under such conditions. Several days later, all of the airmen were rescued, but the planes had to be abandoned. The place where they rested was ever after called Million Dollar Valley, in honor of the presumed value of the downed aircraft. The reason that the pilots had become disoriented was the loss of the radio range from Watson Lake, turned off for a fateful 20 minutes while the generator there was being repaired.[221]

The initial solution was to ferry airplanes to a point where stateside pilots could turn planes over to pilots with more experience in flying under Alaskan conditions. The flow of planes began to increase with most of the planes being P-40 fighters and transports plus enough B-26s to replace those lost on the route in January.

But little materiel could be transported by military aircraft, leading the Army to contract with commercial airlines. The Canadians were concerned that such flights would cause the unauthorized inroads of American carriers in Canada, but the Army said the planes would carry only military supplies and nothing that could be deemed commercial. This flurry was one of the opening rounds in the conflict between American military necessity and Canada's long-standing concern about its sovereignty. Military transports were added, and supplies were flown both up the West Coast and over the NWSR.[222]

The Army feared that a Japanese attack on Alaska could happen at any time and tried to get many planes there as quickly as possible. Because such an attack did not take place immediately, more fighters and bombers, including some B-17s, the famous Flying Fortress, were flown in without great difficulty.

The first day of the Japanese attack on the Aleutians, the invaders were able to operate unmolested thanks to protective weather conditions. But the next day, June 4, 1942, the Aleutian Tigers, a squadron led by Maj. Jack Chenault, son of the famous aviator Claire Chenault, brought down three Japanese planes with the loss of two of his own. The Americans were learning on the job about the superiority of the Mitsubishi Zero. Meanwhile, bombers of the 11th Air Force attacked the Japanese carriers without, however, scoring any direct hits. In response to the attack on the Aleutians, the Royal Canadian Air Force sent a squadron to help, the first of five such Canadian units, although they were forced to complain before they were allowed to join in the combat flying against the Japanese.[223]

Air war over the Aleutians was unsatisfactory for the Japanese, the Americans and the Canadians, because their common enemy was the weather, characterized by heavy fog. But the defenders were able to pin down the Japanese and make it impossible for them to advance from their positions at Kiska and Attu.

Not only had the NWSR contributed to the defense of Alaska, but the Japanese threat there had demonstrated the value of an inland supply route. The Army moved its air supply headquarters inland from Seattle to Great Falls, Montana. During the summer the pace of flights increased, and for a few months the Army literally commandeered commercial airplanes for transport duty.[224] On many of these flights, pilots could watch the Alcan Highway begin to snake across the land.

As for the supposed link between the Alcan Highway and the NWSR, the planes were using the airway long before even the pioneer road was completed. The threat of Japanese invasion was too great, and the Alaska garrison was too weak to wait. During 1942, some 311 aircraft were delivered over the NWSR, and only a few of the pilots had the benefit of the Alcan Highway track on the ground to guide them, but they would come to give it high praise. Said one pilot: "While it was not the mission of the American and Canadian road builders, military and civilian, to give ferry pilots a navigational aid, I cannot overemphasize how vital that road was to us to do the job we were assigned."[225] That was especially true for pilots forced to land on it.

From 1942 through the end of the war, 716 planes would be delivered over the NWSR for the Air Corps in Alaska. In addition, between 35 and 40 commercial aircraft, operating under military control, flew almost 80 million ton-miles and more than 370 million passenger miles in support of Alaska defense, in ever-increasing annual amounts.[226] The NWSR had delivered the aircraft that would be essential to mounting a defense of the Aleutians when the Japanese attacked. In meeting these purposes, it was one of the most timely and effective defensive measures taken at the start of the war. Yet its secondary function, as a major route for the supply of aircraft to the Soviet Union, would dwarf its original purpose. More than ten times as many planes for the Soviet Union than for Alaska would pass over the NWSR.

By late 1942, talks between the United States and the U.S.S.R. had progressed to a point where deliveries of planes could begin over Alsib, the Army's name for the Alaska-Siberia Lend Lease delivery program. Despite numerous attempts by the Americans, Stalin had resisted all efforts to have U.S. personnel deliver the planes to European Russia. He had insisted on an American delivery point, so that Soviets would fly them home keeping to the north of Japan, and avoiding any threat to its neutrality, which might be caused if Americans piloted the planes. The aircraft would be turned over to the Soviets at Ladd Field in Fairbanks, would refuel at Nome and then continue to Siberia.

Despite the urgent Soviet need for the planes, Alsib could hardly get off the ground. The Soviets were not ready. Three of the Siberian bases, including the first landfall for the planes from Nome, were rudimentary and barely able to handle the first flights. A Soviet military organization to handle ferry operations had not been created, though there had been long months of negotiations during which there had been time to prepare. One was hastily assembled.

Even more of a problem was continued Soviet ambivalence about the route. On September 3, 1941, the first Lend Lease planes landed at Ladd, as did the advance party of the Soviet mission. As communications and other problems were being ironed out, the Soviet military representative in Washington announced on September 19 that Alsib could not be used. The War Department immediately stopped the flow of planes to Alaska and, on October 4, officially dropped Alsib. Finally, the Soviets changed course for the last time, and authorized the route. By then, Lend Lease planes had been diverted to other uses, making it possible to deliver only relatively few planes more than a year after they had first been requested.[227]

In Siberia, five airfields had been built in 10 months, something of a record for the bureaucracy-ridden Soviet Union, which usually required years for such projects. Unlike the NWSR, with airfields no more than 300 miles apart, the Soviets placed their bases as much as 800 miles apart on the 3,500-mile route. The planes were flown slowly across Siberia in order to conserve fuel, meaning that Russian pilots spent long hours in unheated aircraft flying at low altitudes.

The tough flying conditions took their toll on both Americans and Soviets. On the American portion, 59 planes or less than 1 percent were lost on their way from Montana to Alaska with 15 airmen killed. The Soviets claimed about the same safety rate, with only 73 planes lost over Siberia with a reported loss of 112 lives.[228] Some planes encountered difficulties on the way to Nome, involving the loss of 13 lives. The Soviets had refused to accept planes unless they were in top condition, ready for winter, because they had no service facilities at the Siberian bases, and these high acceptance standards probably reduced losses.

While Alsib took place behind the battle lines, it was still part of the wider war, and that fact was occasionally brought home to the pilots. The aircraft were sensitive equipment and vulnerable to silent sabotage. Pilots reported finding fuel lines hammered loose and acid injected into parachutes so they would deteriorate. Fuel was doctored. The FBI sent agents to Alaska, disguised as enlisted Army personnel. While the sabotage seemed to have been carried out by Nazi sympathizers, they were unorganized and amateur. Still, the damage they inflicted simply added to the complexity of the task.

Despite some good working relationships between the Soviets and Americans, tension ran high and the kind of allied partnership that developed with soldiers of other nations did not occur in Alaska. On the American side, there was continued dislike of Communism, a subject generally avoided in conversation, and an eagerness to learn as much as possible about the secretive Soviet Union. On the Soviet side, historical mistrust of foreigners was compounded by a sense that the relationship with the United States was only an expedient and not based on a truly long-term, common interest.

On July 15, 1943, an incident occurred, which showed the distrust underlying the relationship. Two Soviet intelligence officers asked for a driver to take them to a nearby lake where they wanted to relax. Their driver, Pvt. John O. White, had been a Fairbanks taxi driver and knew the way, parked and waited. After the Soviet officers returned to the car, they could not find White. When they located a phone and called for help, they said they were afraid that White "had been drowned" in a lake. A search revealed only a neat pile of his clothing at the edge of the lake.

Finally, the Soviet officers admitted that they had been burning classified documents in the woods and had also been hunting ducks, a violation of Alaska game laws. On July 26, after the Army had almost completely pumped the lake dry, White's body was found, but with no sign of foul play. White had not known how to swim, and rumors that he had been murdered circulated. Yet the Army abruptly stopped any further investigation of the Soviet officers, and the mystery of White's death was never solved.[229]

The most curious charge against the Soviets was that they were using Alsib to carry on espionage. It was likely that some of the sealed, diplomatic luggage traveling northward contained consumer goods on their way to Russia, but some soldiers thought they contained something more. The diplomatic luggage volume increased and was accompanied by armed guards. One American officer insisted on searching some of the sealed luggage, and finally succeeded with the help of an armed U.S. sentry. He said that he had found scientific papers, road and railway maps of the United States and secret military documents, some labeled "Manhattan Military District," the code name for the project developing the atomic bomb.[230] Nobody ever knew with certainty if the Soviets were shipping the fruits of their espionage, but their protective attitude and obvious hostility to questions about what they were doing enhanced American suspicions about Alsib's possibly hidden purpose.

The United States produced 14,798 aircraft for delivery to the Soviet Union under Lend Lease. Some 690 were lost on the way to delivery points, and 7,924 were delivered at Fairbanks with the remainder going by other routes. As they came through the airway, the white American star was replaced by the Soviet red star, actually a copy of the Texaco red-star logo, the only pattern American service personnel could find. The total Lend Lease aircraft supply amounted to about 12 percent of the Soviet Air Force, and more than half of that supply came through Alsib. Almost all of the American planes went to Europe, but at the end of the war, some 543 were diverted to the Soviet Far East.

Most of the planes delivered at Fairbanks were fighters, designed for close support of ground operations. Although Stalin had asked for four-engine bombers, the Soviets received only light and medium bombers, two-engine planes. More than 700 transport planes and a few trainers were also sent.[231]

The annual rate of supply kept increasing as the Soviets grew stronger and took the offensive, although Stalin continually complained that deliveries were behind schedule. Still, in 1944, the U.S.S.R. received 3,148 planes, while only 128 were delivered for use in Alaska.[232]

With the end of the war in Europe in May 1945, Lend Lease aid to the Soviet Union, not yet at war with Japan, was immediately cut off. The Soviets were furious, because they had been given no advance notice, no matter how clear the logic. Because Stalin had agreed to enter the war against Japan, the Americans calmed him by providing assurances that promised supplies would continue to support that war effort. The Soviets still grumbled. Two days after the United States dropped the first atomic bomb but exactly on the day he had previously promised to declare war against Japan, Stalin entered the war in Asia. Perhaps the United States, by not pressing for early Soviet intervention, had decided to keep the Soviet Union out of the occupation of the home islands, though the Soviets would acquire some Japanese territory. With the Japanese surrender, Lend Lease finally ended.

Once the war was over, animosity between the United States and the Soviet Union grew so virulent that Lend Lease was soon pushed aside as if it had been a bad dream. Harry Hopkins went to Moscow to discuss compensation owed to the United States and found that Stalin considered the termination of Lend Lease "unfortunate and brutal."

Stalin told him that he had "intended to make a suitable expression of gratitude to the United States for lend-lease assistance during the war, but the way in which the program had been halted made that impossible now."[233] The Soviet Union had received $11 billion or 22 percent of Lend Lease assistance, second only to Great Britain. By 1960, all recipients except the Soviet Union had made settlements on what they owed, with the United States receiving more than $10 billion. Only after the collapse of the Soviet Union and Russia's need for American help did it agree in 1990 to repay $674 million. All of the Lend Lease funds had, in fact, been spent in the United States with the aim of winning the war, so full compensation had never been contemplated.

Just as they had been parsimonious with cash, so were the Soviets loath to praise the American effort. Gratitude gave way to denial. General M.G. Machin, the Soviet head of Alsib, had received the U.S. Legion of Merit, one of the U.S. Army's highest decorations, but he was "advised" not to wear it in public. Soviet propaganda suggested that the importance of American aid had been exaggerated and implied that it had been unnecessary. Only after the fall of the Soviet Union did the Russians admit that the Americans had supplied the equivalent of 250 air regiments.

Despite its success, the NWSR proved to be a major irritant in United States relations with Canada, reflecting the persistent American inability to understand its neighbor. The issues between them embodied the conflict between the American view that it was using Canadian territory and facilities to fight a war in their common interest and the Canadian concern that its much larger neighbor was using its dominant presence in parts of the country to lay the basis for the long-term economic and possibly political domination of Canada.

The most public example of this conflict was the use of Northwest Airlines equipment and staff to transport military supplies and personnel to and from Alaska. Despite its protests about the initial, illegal Northwest flight in February 1942 and American promises that commercial carriers would be militarized, Northwest continued to fly using its own insignias and uniforms. Canada was determined to allow no American commercial aviation to displace its own growing airlines and protested strongly. Over Northwest's objections, the War Department insisted that markings on its planes be changed and that its personnel either be drafted or required to wear military-type uniforms. Northwest gradually complied.[234] Later, Canada found that Air Transport Command planes were carrying commercial passengers to fill empty seats, leading to a new round of negotiations in which it was finally able to protect Canadian traffic, while allowing the ATC service to continue. The Americans seemed to think at each juncture that the Canadian Government had been satisfied with arrangements but failed to understand that suspicion was growing about U.S. postwar intentions.

Another test of wills arose over responsibility for construction along the NWSR. On principle, Canada did not want another country investing in facilities with permanent and lasting value, such as airports, because it did not want to create the basis for any postwar claims to a right to use those facilities. It insisted on building the NWSR airfields, and Canadian labor backed the Government, believing that it had been allowed only a small part of the work on the Alcan Highway. In April 1942, the Canadian Government had said that it would allow the Americans to pay only for improvements above Canadian standards. The work would be done by Canadian labor and the facilities would be owned by Canada.

The Americans were dissatisfied by the pace of construction and pressed for the authority to build the needed facilities. The PJBD's Recommendation 29, adopted on February 24, 1943, called for new construction to be carried out by Americans, although Canadian workers might be used. The Canadian Government did not approve it, despite mounting pressure from the Americans who argued that expanded facilities were urgently needed. This was one of only two PJBD wartime recommendations not approved, both times by Canadian refusal.

The first sign of retreat came in June 1943, when the Canadians authorized the Americans to build temporary facilities, but not those which would survive the war. Later that month, faced with the scope of the projects, well beyond Canadian capabilities, they authorized construction by Americans except at Edmonton. By 1944, Canada returned to its original policy of doing the work, but allowed the United States to carry out work at two airfields.[235] The Government also decided that it would repay the Americans for any permanent facilities they had built, then estimated as requiring a payment of $31 million, but ultimately reaching about $80 million.

Finally, the Canadians were concerned about control of air space and of facilities on the ground. Under a PJBD recommendation, it moved toward a satisfactory level of air traffic control on the NWSR and easily recovered full control of its airways when the war ended. Another PJBD recommendation gave Canada clear control over all of the major airfields between Edmonton and Whitehorse, while placing the temporary, emergency air strips under U.S. control.[236]

From the beginning and to the end of the NWSR, despite its overwhelming use by the Americans, the project retained a Canadian character. While it turned out to have much less postwar value than the Canadians had believed, they could take pride in the sponsorship of a successful joint operation. With the end of the war and Alsib, the NWSR fell into disuse. Soon longer-range aircraft would fly directly to Alaska without multiple stops. The defense of Alaska would no longer depend on the route over the Alaska Highway.

CHAPTER 8.

THE GREATEST WASTE: CANOL

The same panic and lack of good intelligence about Japan's capabilities that had led to the hasty decision to build the Alcan Highway caused another reflexive reaction at about the same time. In late April 1942, the War Department decided to build a pipeline in the deepest Canadian Northwest to supply fuel to trucks and airplanes on the Alcan Highway and the NWSR. Unlike the Alcan Highway, which became the stuff of military legend, and NWSR, which quietly got its job done, the pipeline – called Canadian Oil or simply Canol – was destined to be a costly and controversial failure.

Just as Alaska seemed vulnerable and threatened with being cut off from the urgently needed supply of aircraft, weapons and war personnel, it might also find itself without a reliable fuel supply if the Japanese were successful in disrupting West Coast ocean routes. At the January 16, 1942 Cabinet meeting, Roosevelt expressed his concern to both the War and Navy Secretaries about this possible vulnerability and the looming shortage of tankers, which were being sunk by enemy submarines. Traditional Pacific supply sources in the Dutch East Indies were falling to the Japanese, and even Caribbean refineries were subject to shelling from German U-boats.[237]

Beyond the need to consider how to supply Alaska, especially difficult because of the lack of good information about Japan's real capabilities, was the problem of fueling vehicles that would be using the Alcan Highway and airplanes refueling along the NWSR. While there were substantial known oil reserves in Alaska, they were not readily accessible and no significant drilling had yet occurred. Finally, Arctic explorer Vilhjalmur Stefansson kept pressing the Army to look to the North. He had unsuccessfully advocated an Alcan Highway route, which would have run far to the north of the actual track of the road, but he was not deterred.

To be successful surviving in the Canadian North, a person must be tough and persistent, so despite the rejection of his proposed Alcan Highway route, he stayed around Washington, becoming an advisor to Col. William "Wild Bill" Donovan, whose new intelligence operation would become the fabled OSS — Office of Strategic Services –forerunner of the Central Intelligence Agency. Stefansson told Donovan that there was already a functioning oil field at Norman Wells, in Canada's Northwest Territory, with its own small refinery. Because of the high paraffin content of the oil, it had a pour point of 90 below, so it would not have to be warmed in order to flow through a pipeline. The War Department began to consider that Norman Wells could be developed even without the Alcan Highway itself being routed to pass it.

When the Cabinet met in April 2, 1942, after work on the Alcan Highway had begun, Harold Ickes, a close political confidant of the President serving both as Secretary of the Interior and Petroleum Administrator for War, raised the issue of fuel supply for Alaska and advocated stepped up oil exploration there. But Ickes and Secretary of War Stimson did not explore the suggestion further in the weeks following the Cabinet session. Instead, the Army pushed ahead with its own plans, now heavily influenced by Stefansson, a Canadian who not surprisingly was pushing a Canadian, not an Alaskan, solution to the fuel problem. The Army appeared to be indifferent to the benefit that might accrue to Canada from helping it develop its oil reserves.

Stefansson contacted Imperial Oil of Canada, a subsidiary of Standard Oil of New Jersey, better known as Esso, which had developed the small project at Norman Wells to supply the local population. While the potential output of the oilfield was unknown, it would certainly be large enough to provide supplies well in excess of the local demand of 450 barrels a day, perhaps going as high as 5,000. The explorer proposed a route to bring the oil out using a 300-mile pipeline and river barges.

Lt. Gen. Somervell, the Army's logistics chief, assigned James H. Graham, his assistant, to make a recommendation on the proposal. Graham had been a supply officer in World War I and was Dean of the University of Kentucky School of Engineering. Although he had worked for an oil company during his career, he was not an expert on either finding or transporting oil. He talked sporadically with Army personnel during April 1942, learning that Standard Oil of New Jersey was somewhat dubious about the feasibility of the project. Finally, on April 29, 1942, what would turn out to be the only meeting ever held to plan the pipeline took place in the office Brig. Gen. A.H. Carter, the officer in charge of the Army's budget. Stefansson was not invited, and neither was any representative of the Corps of Engineers. The Petroleum Administrator for War or his representative was also notably absent.

Carter went along with Stefansson's projections and said that the Army could use as much as 5,000 barrels a day. The Standard Oil and Imperial representatives said that no less than 45 new wells would have to be put into operation just to reach 3,000 barrels. The Army had decided that the refinery should be located at Whitehorse, meaning that a pipeline almost 600 miles long would have to be built to bring the oil from Norman Wells. On Graham's recommendation, the group decided that a 4-inch pipeline, a small diameter even in the 1940s, would be used, because the pipe was available and could handle as much as 5,000 barrels a day. Finally, the group agreed that a small, older refinery, yet to be found, should be dismantled in the United States and transported to Whitehorse. Any such refinery was, at the time, under the jurisdiction of the Petroleum Administrator. No minutes were made of the meeting.

Now Imperial moved to strike a hard bargain, mostly because it had no interest in expanding the Norman Wells oilfield, building the pipeline or assembling the refinery. The oilmen warned the group about the lack of adequate transportation routes to get the pipe and drilling equipment to Norman Wells, implying that considerable time would be required to get the project done. The United States would have to pay for the project, and Imperial would get the residual rights to it.

After the meeting, Graham immediately prepared a brief memo with recommendations for action by Somervell. Without any supporting information, the memo proposed that Somervell order the Engineers, previously excluded from the discussions, to have Imperial drill at least nine wells by September 1942, create a supply route ready for operation by October 1, 1942. Somervell immediately approved Graham's recommendations. The next day, he ordered the Corps of Engineers to "take the necessary steps to carry out these recommendations at the earliest practicable date."[238] The last words might suggest that Somervell recognized that the memo's deadlines were impossible to beat, but his actions suggest that he might have hoped he could do even better.

This rush to decide, without any detailed studies, overriding the qualms of the oil companies and excluding the Petroleum Administrator, in whose area of responsibility such a project would fall, suggests that Graham's discussions and his recommendations supported a decision that Somervell had already made. Somervell enjoyed almost unlimited power, having risen rapidly to his position over many generals with greater seniority. His greatest achievement on his way to the top was the construction of the Pentagon, then the world's largest building. He had shown he could get a job done and could work quickly, but even he acknowledged that he had little regard for budgetary restraints. By April 1942, he was fully in charge of logistics and full of both self-confidence and self-importance. Somervell got what he wanted, but he was not popular. "As the stories of Somervell's temper and vindictiveness spread, so did the number of his enemies,"[239] reported Twichell.

The process of selecting the companies to perform the actual work reflected both the haste that Somervell had imposed on the project and the U.S. Government's ability to play favorites among the players carrying out defense contracts. On the same day it received Somervell's orders, the Chief of the Corps of Engineers designated his deputy, Maj. Gen Thomas M. Robins, to carry out the required tasks. Robins opposed the project, saying that "ten times the volume of deliveries contemplated by the pipe line could be made by barges already available from inland United States rivers, and at one-tenth of the cost and effort."[240] But he said nothing to Somervell and followed orders. Somervell heard from others in the Army that they thought the plan ill-advised, but left his orders unchanged.

On May 1, 1942, the War Department reached an agreement with Imperial, almost entirely on the oil company's terms. Robins informed the State Department that it should obtain the Canadian Government's agreement, but did not refer the matter to the PJBD, which would never be asked to make any recommendation on the need for the project. Presumably, because that body considered matters and then made recommendations for action by the two countries, Somervell believed that using the PJBD would cause unacceptable delays. Besides, the Army regarded the decision as already having been made by the United States.

W.A. Bechtel Company, a privately held California company, which was already building ships as part of the war effort, would be the contractor. There would be no bid process, because once again that process would take too much time. Somervell met with Stephen D. Bechtel, Sr., and convinced the contractor by offering a cost-plus contract yielding a 10 percent profit margin and the right to select his own subcontractors.

Somervell placed only one condition on the deal: that Bechtel would keep it secret so that Ickes would not find out about the Canol project. Bechtel, who had had some run-ins with Ickes, readily agreed. Somervell was worried that Ickes would either take control of Canol or kill it. While Ickes' authority did not extend to Canada, he was supposed to control pipe and refineries in the U.S. Thus, he could effectively stop the project by refusing to allow the needed components to be moved out of the country. To protect against either threat from Ickes, Somervell told Bechtel that he had secreted an appropriation of $25 million, enough to get Canol well under way, in a war appropriations bill. Actually he waited until hearings were completed and, on May 6, 1942, added the amount without any explanation.

Bechtel lined up H.C. Price Co., Texas pipeline builders, and W.E. Callahan Construction Co., as its subcontractors. Many people in Canada would think BPC, as the triumvirate was known, was a single company and, in effect, it was, because Bechtel ran the show. Somervell's discussions with Bechtel appear to have taken place before April 29, when the Graham recommendations were submitted, further supporting the notion that Dean Graham's memo was window dressing for a decision already made. The deal with Bechtel was made on May 4 and on May 6 contracts were given to the architect-engineers. All contracts were cost-plus arrangements with a guaranteed margin for the contractors no matter what happened.

Later in May, at Bechtel's urging, the War Department signed up Standard Oil of California as consultant during construction and as operator. The oil company warned that the construction would take far longer than planned and the volumes of oil might not meet forecasts, but its advice was ignored.

Somervell was an empire builder. Just before launching Canol, he began considering a railway to Alaska. While that plan never materialized, Canol kept growing. The first major change was caused, at least in part, by Ickes. Despite Somervell's efforts, during May Ickes had discovered the project, thanks to his deputy who was a former officer of Standard Oil of California, and he protested to Roosevelt, who provided an answer probably written in the War

Department. According to a later study by Somervell's command, while the President recognized that Ickes might be right about the likelihood of failure of Canol, he stated that "the project has my full approval."[241] Roosevelt's reply suggested once again that "do something, anything" was still the prevailing policy.

The Japanese attack on the Aleutians, making clear that Alaska remained in peril, led Ickes to come up with an alternative. Oil could be shipped by rail to Prince Rupert on the Canadian West Coast, transported from there through the Inland Passage to Skagway and from there by pipeline to Whitehorse. Ickes argued, correctly as it turned out, that such a supply could be put in place well before Canol could be ready, because he believed it would not begin to operate until mid-1943. Both Robins and Standard Oil of California, Somervell's own consultant, had also proposed this route.

By June 1942, only a few weeks after Canol was launched, it became clear even to the Army that the pipeline could not be completed as quickly as Graham had suggested. The Corps of Engineers set a new target date of December 1, 1943, about 14 months behind schedule. That made the Ickes proposal look attractive, and Somervell, instead of dropping his original plan, simply tacked the new proposal onto his first scheme.

In the short life of Canol to this point, between April and June 1942, it had become evident that the project would neither meet Alaska's urgent needs nor supply many of the NWSR airfields. Despite the success of Ickes' route, Somervell went ahead with his plans. While BPC might have the contract to carry out the project, they could not mobilize nearly as quickly as the Corps of Engineers. An Engineer team of three battalions, was assembled and assigned to start the project and to support the civilian contractors as they arrived.

Ickes himself caused some of the delay. Because his proposal could bring refined product to the Alcan Highway, there was really no need for the refinery. For months, he resisted the Army's effort to purchase a small refinery in

Texas, which he claimed was needed for other purposes. He did not relent until November 1942, when it was clear that Somervell would persist with Canol even with fuel flowing freely through Skagway. Thanks to this delay, Somervell harvested the fruit of his earlier attempt to go around Ickes. Even with the multiple supply routes being put in place, the pipeline would not be able to make its December 1943 target. Gasoline flowed through the Skagway-Whitehorse pipeline on January 20, 1943 and the supply to Skagway was never hampered by enemy action. The stated purpose of Canol had been met.

But Somervell had already begun to think big. He ordered a study for supplying refined product to Nome and Anchorage and even as far as the Aleutians.[242] The possible new oil supply led to grandiose strategizing. Suppose Japan attacked the Soviet Union, and the United States had to protect the Soviet Asian flank. Operations would be launched out of Alaska, but would be hamstrung by a shortage of fuel there. More oil had to be found in the North. By September, a contract had been concluded with an American drilling company to wildcat as many 100 new wells in Canada. Undoubtedly, with such plans in mind, Somervell would not consider any change in the plans for Canol. In effect, without any extensive Washington discussions, Canol's mission was substantially changed. The fact that the four-inch line would not be adequate to transport much oil was simply set aside for later consideration.

On Canol, black Engineers, the 388th Battalion, found themselves generally isolated from other troops and outside contacts. When they did meet Canadians, either outpost operators or natives, they found that the local people had been warned about them. One veteran reported that the natives "had been told we had tails."[243] The narrator of a BPC-sponsored film, made for the Army as the construction work went on, commented that "colored Engineer troops developed great skill in handling that pipe without neglecting other skills, of course," while the screen flickered with scenes of troops soft-shoe dancing and shooting craps.[244] No similar "compliment" was paid to the white troops.

Because of the Army's initial optimism about getting the supply route completed quickly, the soldiers did not begin to receive cold-weather gear until October, more than a month after winter had begun. Diesel and gasoline froze solid as winter deepened. Although the troops eventually built some sled-borne shelters for themselves, many remaining in tents, which could easily be moved as construction progressed. In sharp contrast, BPC workers were spared the tent accommodations and almost always had warm accommodations and a roof over their heads. The soldiers resented the distinctions between the two groups, especially the much higher pay that the civilians received.

All of this activity, far beyond the scope of the original NWSR and Alcan Highway plans, took place without Washington paying much attention to the fact that the construction was almost all in somebody else's country. The Army seemed to believe that it had a blank check to do whatever it deemed necessary. Just as Somervell had ignored objections to his Canol plans, the Army simply rolled over Canada, believing America's northern neighbor could be bought off.

After the State Department notified the Canadian Government on May 1, 1942, of the Canol decision, the Canadians expressed the same doubts about its usefulness as had been voiced by Standard Oil and many others. The American Government, persistently putting pressure on Ottawa, stressed that Somervell had structured the deal so that Canada would end up owning facilities built and paid for by Americans. All of the new wells drilled by Imperial would belong to Imperial, which would sell crude oil to the Army at contract prices, guaranteeing it a handsome profit.

The State Department agreed with the Canadians that the project did not make economic sense. But it believed that, if the project were to go forward, the Army's planning was deficient, because it did not require keeping the pipeline and refinery in place after the war in case of another war. However, the U.S. Minister to Canada believed that Canada would never agree to any limitations on what it might do in its own territory after the war, in effect lending support to the Army's approach. Finally, in late June 1942, the Canadian Government agreed to the construction of the pipeline and refinery. The Canadians continued to express their doubts about the entire project, and U.S. Minister to Canada J. Pierrepont Moffat reported his view that the investment of large sums in Canada for this purpose embittered him, an unusually strong statement for a diplomat.

When the Army began building the string of airfields and a winter road to Norman Wells without even informing them, the Canadians were furious. Hugh Keenleyside, a top official of the Ministry of External Affairs and a member of the PJBD, told Moffat that "it is very important that we should be informed first, as soon as the United States authorities began to discuss any new projects in the field. They can think as much as they like in Washington, but the minute the matter becomes a subject of conversation among American officers in Canada it is bound to become known to the Canadians in the area...."[245] When informed of American drilling plans, the Canadian Oil Controller, Ickes's northern counterpart, reported: "I am in complete ignorance."[246]

The result of the Canadian protest was that the wildcatting plan was submitted to Canada for its approval, although well after the contract had been signed with the drilling company. By January 13, 1943, Canada formally agreed. The profits from any of the new wells would be shared equally by Imperial, still the subsidiary of a U.S. company, and the Canadian Government, and the wells themselves would become Imperial's property after the war.

Somervell essentially got what he wanted and, for the time being, so did the Canadians. Because of their preoccupation with the war in Europe, where a large Canadian contingent had been committed, the Canadians were content with being informed in advance of U.S. intentions and with agreements that insured that American commercial interests would not gain a postwar foothold in Canada as a result of the U.S. Government's wartime investment there. On the same day as Canada agreed to wildcatting in the Yukon and a portion of the Canadian Northwest, the PJBD adopted a recommendation that all U.S. "immovable defense installations" would become Canadian or provincial government property within a year after the war, and that the Americans' other property could either be removed from Canada, sold to the Canadians or, if neither, sold in the open market. This recommendation was quickly approved by both governments.[247]

The pipeline was completed on February 16, 1944, and crude oil finally flowed to the refinery, on which work had begun a year earlier, in April 1944. In its 11 months of operation, the old Texas refinery would receive about one million barrels of crude, the equivalent of a small fleet of tanker trucks each day. Meanwhile, fuel from the Skagway route had reached Watson Lake on a 2-inch line in June 1943 and Fairbanks, on a 3-inch line, in November 1943.

By the time the refinery was closed in early April 1945, it had produced 311,000 barrels of aviation fuel, gasoline and diesel.[248] These quantities of fuel could have been transported in a single tanker. The cost of a gallon of gasoline originating at Norman Wells was $7.72 ($89.55) compared with the wartime civilian price, regarded as high, of $0.29 ($3.36). After it was closed, Imperial bought the refinery and moved it. The pipe was sold for scrap, except for Canol 2, which continued to operate to transport refined product. The project cost $134 million ($1.554 billion) exclusive of the Army's direct costs. If it were the same proportion of the Federal budget as it had been during World War II, in 2004 it would have amounted to $8 billion, almost exactly the same as the Highway. After the war, it took many years before it proved economical to find and transport oil from Norman Wells to outside markets.

Canada never realized any reward from Canol's "immovable defense installations", other than the ability to import supply from Skagway. Even more importantly,

Canol made no real contribution to the defense effort and probably drew men, materiel and money away that could have been better used elsewhere. The Canadian Government gained large U.S. dollar reserves from the money spent by the Americans, and the private companies, especially Bechtel and its associates and Imperial, profited handsomely.

In one respect the Canol project was perfect: it was a textbook case of government waste.

PART IV. PAYING THE PRICE

CHAPTER 9.

WHY GO THE EXTRA MILE?

On February 17, 1942, President Roosevelt answered a reporter's news conference question: "I was about to ask whether in your opinion the Air Force as it stands, and the Navy as it stands in the Pacific, are sufficient to deal with anything." Roosevelt replied: "No. Certainly not."[249]

Roosevelt had just told the press that he could not give "any assurance" that Alaska would not be attacked that year. Just three days earlier, he had made an address to the Canadian people, denying any competitive interest and urging more joint effort.[250] Clearly worried about continental defense, he supported the urgent construction of a supply route to Alaska. In early 1942, the purpose of the Alcan effort, then a string of airfields and soon a pioneer road, was justified by a fear of vulnerability.

Alcan had a clear mission, and both of the 1942 projects moved the United States toward a reasonable, strategic objective. Yet not everybody believed, even then, that the road was necessary.

The Navy maintained that it could supply Alaska by sea, even in the face of possible Japanese submarine attacks on merchant vessels, such as had occurred in the months immediately following Pearl Harbor. By mid-1942, little damage was being done to West Coast shipping, and there was no interruption in the flow of Engineer regiments and supplies for the northern half of the road through Skagway and Valdez. And, as hard as the calculation might be, the occasional loss of a merchant vessel, had it occurred, is likely to have been less costly in both lives and supplies than using the road. The facts ended up supporting the Navy, because for the period between Pearl Harbor and November 1942, the only way heavy supplies could reach Alaska was by ship.

At the same time, the Canadians never overcame their skepticism about the road. It could not help them protect their own coast, because its route was to be far inland. Despite the fall of Singapore in February 1942, shocking to Canadians because of the heavy losses their forces suffered there, their military did not expect a Japanese landing on their territory. Even though the proposed road might support the string of NWSR airfields they had built, they obviously did not believe such support was essential. After all, the airfields had been built without the Alcan Highway. Roosevelt's February 14 speech could easily be viewed on the northern side of the border as lobbying for the Canadian members of the PJBD to acquiesce the next week in American demands for the road. In fact, the Canadians agreed to the road at that meeting, not for strategic reasons, but because they wanted to accommodate the Americans, and they would get a new road for no cost.

Even Roosevelt was unsure about the plans. While his generals dispatched engineers to survey the route, he did not even know if there would be one. At his press conference, he said that "if there is going to be anything accomplished that would be useful by January, 1943, something would have to be done in the next couple of weeks...." Would that "something" be a road? Roosevelt replied:

> It has been suggested that for the immediate needs of this war it would be more practical to build a — a light, one track railway — easier to keep open in the winter.... Another suggestion is that it would be more practical to send things up the inland passage to the end of the inland passage and then a highway from there on. And others have said it would be easier to do the whole thing by transport planes, instead of building a highway. I am speaking in terms of military needs of this year [1942], and possibly the beginning of next year. Well, I don't — I could not

prognosticate what they [the War Department] will
do, if anything...."[251]

The Commander-in-Chief was not sure anything would
be done to link Alaska to the Lower 48. And he had not
wanted publicly to reject the Navy's position that it could
deliver the goods through the inland passage. But the decision was now in the hands of the War Department, and
Roosevelt would simply be a consumer of their conclusions.

The decision to build the pioneer road was actually tan-
tamount to betting that the Navy was correct, and that
Alaska could be supplied by the inland passage during the
critical year of 1942. No matter how fast the Engineers
worked, leaving transport to the merchant fleet was the only
immediately available solution. In effect, the Alcan Highway was insurance against the possibility that the sea route
would turn out to be vulnerable to Japanese submarines.
Buying that insurance was prudent in light of the well-docu-
mented sightings of the subs not far from the West Coast
until well into 1942.

Siting the route was a completely different matter, and
this decision was heavily influenced by earlier military
determinations made by the PJBD. Once the Canadians
acquiesced in the building of a road, it made sense to route it
along the NWSR. The strongest reasons were the presence
of some rudimentary trails, used in connection with the
original construction of some of the airfields and the potential value of the road to supply not only Alaska but the
Yukon and the airfields themselves. There is no evidence
that, in January and February 1942, the War Department
believed that the reason for building Alcan Highway was to
support the airfields, but there is ample support for the routing having been determined by the location of the NWSR
airfields. The distinction between the decision to build the
road and the decision on its site would later be lost in the
quest to justify it.

Intelligence about Japanese intentions was virtually
non-existent early in 1942. While the United States knew
that an attack was likely in December 1941, it had no idea
where. After the Doolittle raid in April, the massive amount

of Japanese radio traffic from vessels trying to find the launch carrier yielded considerable data on the Japanese naval codes. In May, the Navy once again learned that there would a Japanese attack, perhaps on Hawaii or possibly even the West Coast. Commander Joseph J. Rochefort, head of the "Hypo" cryptographic unit at Pearl Harbor that was busy breaking the Japanese naval code, thought that "AF," the Japanese target, would actually be Midway Island. The Navy code personnel in Washington, at the time locked in a bureaucratic turf battle with Rochefort, rejected his finding.

Rochefort came up with a scheme for proving Hypo's theory. He sent a message by undersea cable to Midway, asked them to send an uncoded radio message that the island's desalination plant had broken down. Within two days, Tokyo Naval Intelligence, using their now-broken naval code, sent a signal that AF's distillation plant was broken and that it would run out of water in two weeks. The final piece of the code that Hypo had broken revealed the date of the attack.[252]

The Navy finally believed him, and Rochefort's work led to the American victory at Midway, after which the Japanese were never again to launch an offensive operation in the Pacific. Other than its last seaplane bombing of Oregon in September, it would never attack any military or naval target on the West Coast. Better yet, the Navy would now know of Japanese plans in advance. The Japanese invasion of the Aleutians, intended as the diversionary piece of the Battle of Midway, brought increased American naval surveillance of the North Pacific and yielded good intelligence showing that the Japanese had pulled the Imperial Navy back from the West Coast.

The War Department seems not to have known of the Navy's intelligence breakthrough. The Army probably knew that, by November 1942, the United States had no operational aircraft carriers in the Pacific. However, the year's naval battles had been so devastating that neither the Americans nor the Japanese would be able to launch any serious naval attacks until 1944.

The course of the war was beginning to turn. On November 30, 1942, Churchill had said: "This is not the end, it is not even the beginning of the end. But it is, perhaps, the end of the beginning."[253] Whatever the Navy knew and whatever Churchill said, the Army did not reconsider its Alcan Highway policy. Neither improved intelligence nor a better strategic understanding of the war could change the course of a project that by now had its own momentum.

Had the Army chosen to reconsider the Alcan Highway at this time, it had realistic options. The winter pioneer road was completed, making the immediate supply of Alaska and the airfields possible. But some of the pioneer road's bridges would easily be torn out by ice flows and some of the road itself would simply melt away when the weather warmed. The supposed greatest engineering feat since the Panama Canal was a good deal less permanent than its predecessor. The PRA contractors would have the job in the spring of building the all-weather Alaska Highway, but most of their workers had been sent home to wait for warmer weather. The depth of winter gave Somervell's newly created Northwest Service Command time to decide on the next steps.

The most obvious question, but one that was never asked, was whether it was necessary to have a through road from Dawson Creek, British Columbia, to Fairbanks. How much freight actually traveled the full length of the road? The road served in bits and pieces, and some of the pieces were not necessary. In short, something less than an all-weather road could serve in some places.

But momentum was dictated less by the Engineers and military concerns than by the civilian PRA. The Alaska Highway was the largest single project it had ever undertaken, and it had assigned its top people to the project. While it was theoretically under the supervision of the Engineers, the PRA was in constant conflict with the Army. In 1943, only after a tough struggle did the Army succeed in reducing the planned construction standards because of the reduced need for the road. But there would be no stopping it.

The actual construction work was not done by the Government agency; it hired contractors to build assigned segments of the road. During the summer of 1943, there were about 30,000 people working on the road and related facilities. The PRA's organization of this effort was chaotic with supplies pouring into construction centers faster than they could be handled. The contractors had little incentive to be efficient as they collected exorbitant rents for their equipment and management fees calculated on the "cost-plus" system, a "contractor's dream."[254] The result pushed project costs well beyond original estimates, with one primary contractor charging more than double the planned budget amount.

To be sure, the PRA contractors had provided essential help in getting the pioneer road completed before the end of 1942, a role for which they received little credit. But the rewards for their 1943 work on a project no longer militarily essential must have eased any hurt feelings.

When the work was completed in 1943, the Army estimated that the highway could transport 720,000 tons a year, if supplies were needed urgently, or about 400,000 tons under normal conditions. These estimates presupposed shipping supplies from one end of the road to the other. The congressional committee investigating the road at the end of the war found that there "has been little movement of freight over the entire length of the highway."[255] In one year, the average haul was less than 360 miles. Only military use of the road was authorized. In 1943, a scant 134,000 tons of freight were transported, 38 percent for construction of the road itself. The next year the tonnage fell to 119,000 tons, with 36 percent for construction. Freight transport began a steady decline as fuel was transported on Ickes' Canol project, which alone accounted for about 60,000 tons a year.[256]

While Alcan Highway was launched because of a perceived threat, persisting with it to completion could obviously not be justified by concerns about Japanese intentions. So it became a project in search of a mission.

The one undeniably successful and valuable portion of
the Alcan complex was the NWSR. Between 1942 and
1945, 8,646 aircraft had been delivered over its airfields,
more than 90 percent of them destined for the Soviet Union.
Many were short-range aircraft that could not have been
flown to Alaska without the NWSR.[257] Dismantling them
and sending them by ship would have been costly and slow.
More than 1,500 flights in 1942 and the first half of 1943
demonstrated that the NWSR could work well without an
all-weather highway. The first disastrous flights in January
1942 had given way to more reliable transport service as
better trained pilots and mechanics were assigned to duty on
the line. The seven principal fields could be readily supplied
with fuel, and only one used any part of the Alcan Highway.

The official Army history of the Alcan Highway hitched
its wagon to this star. The airfields, "and not the insignifi-
cant amount of freight delivered by road to the Alaska
Defense Command, should be the measure of the highway's
wartime usefulness; for the Alaska Highway was designed
for one primary purpose, and that was to facilitate the building of the airfields and serve as a guide path for flyers....[T]he highway and the staging route amply fulfilled
their principal role."[258]

The testimony of the flyers themselves was that the road
had not been designed as a guide path, but was a welcome
aid. If such help was needed, it could have been provided by
a series of towers, because the cold-climate trees did not
grow to great height and would not hide them. Or the pioneer road would have served. The airfields "facilitated" by
the Alcan Highway were the emergency strips demanded by
the Air Corps, not the main fields built largely by the Canadians. The obscure 1946 report of U.S. House of Representatives Committee on Roads would recognize that the
defense of Alaska had been the reason for the road and the
support of the airfields the reason for its routing.[259]

In 1943, American artist Rockwell Kent, known for his
political leanings toward the Soviet Union, made a Christ-
mas drawing of Alcan Highway construction. It was entitled
"Making Things Easier for Santa Claus (The Alcan

Highway).'' Whatever Kent may have meant, the title carried both the message that the road was of more symbolic
than practical use and that it facilitated the outpouring of
American aid to the Soviet Union.

The decision to build Alcan Highway was originally
justified by what appeared to be the Japanese military threat
in the almost total absence of good intelligence about the
enemy's capabilities. Yet, even at his February 1942 press
conference, Roosevelt tried to keep the threat to Alaska in
perspective. While refusing to provide assurances that
Alaska would not be attacked, he also noted: "They can
come in and shell New York tomorrow night, under certain
conditions. They can probably, so far as that goes, drop
bombs on Detroit tomorrow night, under certain conditions."[260] In short, the entire country, even the heartland, was
vulnerable "under certain conditions."

The decision to build the Alaska Highway was not
finally justified because the intelligence gathered by the
Navy could by mid-1942 provide a good picture of Japanese
capabilities. The failure to disseminate this intelligence
where it could be used and the rivalry between the Army
and the Navy led to overblown highway construction, a relatively small mistake in the great scheme of the War.

In some people's minds, the Highway had little to do
with the war itself. Even before construction began and
overcoming its own reservations about the need for the
road, the Army's War Plans Division supported it as a way
to gain a foothold in Canada. It proposed to "take advantage
of the present war to secure the necessary agreements from
Canada to start work now and finish perhaps many years to
come."[261] This sparsely populated area in the Canadian West
could come under American domination, all in the name of
the common defense of the two countries. Perhaps here was
the true strategic mission for the road.

CHAPTER 10.

THE CANOL MESS AND THE RISE OF HARRY TRUMAN

The enemy threat to the United States was perceived as being so grave that the country would spend whatever it took to win. In planning the Alcan Highway and Canol, when it came to money, no questions were asked.

Except by one man.

Following a lack-luster first term, he had just won re-election to the U.S. Senate for a term he would not complete. A Democrat, he had opposed Roosevelt's bid for a third term and had been forced to defeat a primary opponent supported by the President. He was generally thought to be a machine hack, but honest. In early 1941, having heard there was already enormous waste at military installations under construction around the country, Harry S Truman of Missouri got in his car and starting driving to see for himself. No driver, no staff, no expense money. Just Truman.

Truman had been receiving complaints from people in Missouri about the waste and sweetheart deals in the construction of Fort Leonard Wood.[262] He was also concerned about complaints, including those of his colleagues, that contracts were being doled out to a few large contractors and not spread around the country, so that many states got little or none of the defense construction work. In World War I, he had seen waste and had assumed that the military had learned some lessons. He might have known more, as a member of the Military Subcommittee of the Senate Appropriations Committee.[263] But he was no longer sure, so, he later wrote, "I started out from Washington to make a little investigation on my own."[264]

He had no difficulty in finding waste. In the name of national defense, there simply was no apparent control on spending. He found materials lying on the ground, unused and already useless. The work was largely being done on the "cost plus" basis, a method that provided strong incentives for waste. Contractors had no experience. The work was concentrated in a few large corporations, mostly located in the East.[265] "From seventy to ninety percent of the contracts let so far had been concentrated in an area smaller than Missouri,"[266] he said. He also came to be suspicious of "dollar-a-year" businessmen, who volunteered to run Government procurement programs. He found that they remained on the payroll of their private sector employers and "had not been able to divorce their viewpoint completely from that of their former companies...."[267]

When he got back to Washington, he went to see the President, where, somewhat to his surprise, he found a warm greeting, but, like so many others who met with Roosevelt, came away wondering if he had been understood or simply patronized.[268] But he was not deterred, and on February 10, 1941, he took an action that would eventually propel him into the national limelight. He submitted a bill to investigate the awarding of defense contracts.[269]

As a self-educated and serious student of American history, Truman knew he was treading on dangerous ground. During the Civil War, Congress had created a Joint Committee on the Conduct of the War, which insisted on second-guessing Lincoln and his generals.[270] Roosevelt would not agree to such a committee; he did not want his hands tied in any way when it came to the war effort. Truman proposed from the outset not to get involved in military strategy, but to focus on waste and contracts. He immediately gained strong Senate support when he said that it was "a considerable sin" for the War Department to ignore a senator who knew more about the ability of his state's contractors than did the Army.[271]

The bill made its way to a Senate committee under the control of Senator James F. Byrnes, a man who had the President's confidence. Byrnes was apparently ready to pigeonhole the bill until he learned that Rep. E. Eugene Cox of Georgia, an avowed political enemy of the President, was pressing for a similar committee, but with broader jurisdiction. Byrnes reportedly told Roosevelt that he could get "the investigation into friendly hands," and that the Senate could move faster than the House. After Truman promised not to harm defense, a promise which he would keep, Byrnes relented but only agreed to a committee budget of $15,000. The resolution authorizing the Senate Special Committee to Investigate the National Defense Program gave it authority to study the issues that Truman had raised and "such other matters as the committee deems appropriate."[272] It could not produce legislation. For these purposes, the budget was ludicrous, especially in light of the $7 billion appropriation for Lend Lease a week later.

The Truman Committee, as it soon came to be known, had seven members, five Democrats and two Republicans. As one observer said that, with one exception, they were junior senators known for their "unspectacular competence."[273] The exception was Democrat Tom Connally of Texas, put on the committee to keep an eye on the less-experienced members and, as it turned out, to try to blunt some of the criticisms of the military contractors.

But Truman did not need a keeper and quickly became a respected chairman, leading with a firm hand but willingly sharing the limelight. He gained the cooperation of Republicans thanks to his nonpartisan criticism, including taking on the labor unions' role in raising costs. The Republicans, who had belittled him as a machine politician, had begun to change their minds about him even before the committee was authorized. In one debate, Senator Arthur Vandenberg of Michigan, commenting on Truman's ability to substantiate his arguments, had said: "When the Senator from Missouri makes a statement like that we can take it for the truth."[274] Truman had an abiding and somewhat naive faith that, once people knew the facts about any matter, they could easily agree without partisanship. That belief, which he continually tried to follow, earned him the respect of Republicans and Democrats and was money in the bank as Truman started out.

The Attorney General suggested to Truman a lawyer to head his staff.[275] Hugh Fulton, who had an independent streak like Truman's, asked for $9,000 a year, more than half of the budget, and the new Chairman agreed. With Fulton and a borrowed staff, the Committee went to work immediately. Its first targets were the cost-plus contracts which were pushing construction costs far above the original budget estimates.

The Truman Committee soon encountered the man who would be its chief adversary. Lt. Gen. Somervell, the Chief of Services of Supply, had openly said that the committee had been "formed in iniquity for political purposes". He claimed that it was "axiomatic" that time and money could not both be saved.[276] He shared the view of Roosevelt whose principal rule was "speed, speed, speed."[277] He also thought that Truman had formed the committee to retaliate against him for failing to do the Senator from Missouri a favor in the construction program.

Somervell was a man who inspired strongly contrasting sentiments. An efficient, but sometimes brutal, administrator, Somervell was called "dynamite in a Tiffany box"[278] by his friends, while one adversary said he was "a martinet...[who] resented any intrusion or stepping on his toes."[279] While Somervell would later admit that the Truman Committee had saved $250 million on camp construction, he did not assign that accomplishment any great importance. The bottom line for Somervell was that he should be left alone to do his job and that review by the Truman Committee was not legitimate congressional oversight, but harassment and meddling.

In fact, Roosevelt and Somerville on one side and Truman on the other framed the major debate in responding to a national defense emergency. Was it necessary to spend without control in order to put defenses in place quickly? Was waste inevitable to win a war or could some cost containment principles continue to apply, even in times of crisis? Truman would get an almost unique chance to make his point and one of his major battles with Somervell and ultimately with Roosevelt would come over one piece of the Alcan complex. It would be a classic conflict, because, said one Truman aide, the General's attitude "did not impress Senator Truman. He want ahead anyway." [280]

That was the style that Somervell could well understand, because he, too, "went ahead anyway" even as Canol began to be questioned. Not only had he wanted to keep the project secret from Ickes, but also from any other Government agency that might have an interest or responsibility for oil policy, strategy or use. He sited Canol headquarters and refinery in Whitehorse in the Canadian Yukon rather than Fairbanks, which was on American territory and consequently under Ickes control. Although the reason for building Canol was the supposed inability of the Navy to assure the Army that tankers or barges could make it safely to Skagway, neither Somervell nor any of his subordinates actually asked the Navy. The War Production Board, also with clear authority on the matter, was similarly completely ignored.

At first, in 1942, Ickes was alone in criticizing Canol. Under Secretary of War Robert P. Patterson, who saw his job as assisting not controlling the generals, probably dealt with Ickes using Somervell's words. After Somervell's August 1942 trip to the Yukon, where he had heard that the oilfield might be richer than originally thought, Patterson wrote Ickes that, even with the Interior Secretary's proposed Canol route, the possibility of additional oil was "sufficient to justify" the main pipeline and refinery.

While apologists for Somervell and Bechtel, the prime contractor, might believe that all of their troubles were caused by Ickes and that he had set Truman on the Canol case, the Interior Secretary was not alone. How Somervell could have thought that a project of this magnitude could be kept secret is unclear, but perhaps he realized it would become known only after it was too far along to stop. In late 1942, the War Production Board accidentally found out about it and was told by Patterson that the construction was being carried out "for strategic reasons." This term was the magic formula for keeping other agencies from knowing about military projects. One WPB official concluded, however, that if the project was simply unusable, it would be difficult to justify it on strategic grounds, whatever they might be.[281] In March 1943, Donald Nelson, the head of the WPB and the supposed czar of all Government procurement received a report, based on a thorough study, saying that "it is both our right and our duty to insist that the present wastage of scarce materials and equipment be immediately stopped."[282] Such was his power that Somervell was later to come close to having Roosevelt fire Nelson.

Next, investigators from the Budget Bureau studied the background files and conducted a field inspection. In June 1943, the Bureau forecast a $119 million cost for the project and recommended to Stimson that the pipeline and refinery be abandoned unless they were essential to the war effort. Because West Coast shipping was getting through almost unmolested, the Bureau asked that the need for the project be reviewed by the Joint Chiefs of Staff. Were there "strategic reasons" for continuing?

On July 6, 1943, Somervell sent a memo to Marshall, the Army Chief of Staff, for the first time setting out in some detail the reasons for Canol. It was 14 months after he had authorized the project. He asserted that Norman Wells had been selected after "an intensive study of the geology and production record...," when none had been undertaken. He acknowledged a "more favorable strategic situation in the North Pacific area" but argued that more oil supply developed locally would ease pressure on oil supplies elsewhere and on transportation. Finally, he erroneously equated volumes of refined product to be shipped with volumes of crude to be piped from Norman Wells, when refined volumes are actually considerably lower than crude.

In short, Somervell lied and deceived in his report, while admitting there was no strategic value, only a resource allocation advantage, in completing Canol. He estimated the added cost at $38 million, compared with $50 million that would be lost by abandoning the project.

On October 26, 1943, the Joint Chiefs of Staff acted on the memo and decided that the project was "necessary to the war effort."[283] As usual, they gave no detailed support of their decision, coming just after another decision to reduce forces in Alaska. The Budget Bureau request had backfired. Somervell now could operate under the cover of the Joint Chiefs, sharing responsibility with the top Army and Navy brass, and, in practice, nobody could overturn their decision.

But, before this decision, the Truman Committee had begun investigating Canol. By now, Truman had become a major Washington figure thanks to the previous work of the Committee. On March 8, 1943, Truman had been on the cover of *Time*. The magazine called the Committee "the watchdog, spotlight, conscience and spark plug to the economic war-behind-the-lines" and cited Truman for being "scrupulously honest."[284] Reports about Truman in the media revealed astonishment that the man previously considered little more than a machine hack had turned out to be perhaps the top senator. In a 1944 poll of Washington correspondents, he would be rated as one of the top ten Washington people important to the war effort, the only member of Congress on the list.[285]

A subcommittee visited the Yukon in September, accompanied by an Army "minder", the military's agent assigned to keep an eye on the politicians. Even he came to see this project was indefensible. The Army knew it was in trouble. On October 17, 1943, a Col. Wilde of Somervell's staff phoned to tell Gen. Worsham, the Engineer in charge in the Yukon, that he would need to justify $25 million in spending for the Truman Committee.

Worsham:	On this project, we were instructed in the beginning that there wouldn't be any cost kept.
Wilde:	We've got to prove now exactly what we've done with the money.
Worsham:	I just don't see how reasonable men, when they're this far along, can afford to quit.
Wilde:	That's the point. They're not reasonable. We're in a spot now where all we're trying to do, even if they do stop us, is justify and prevent our trial.[286]

Here were two frightened officers, fearing that they could be held responsible for spending public funds without any accounting at all.

In November 1943, the subcommittee held closed hearings, and late in the month the full Committee began public hearings, where Truman's predilection for the facts would be satisfied. Still, Truman was a loyal ex-soldier, and he hoped to avoid a confrontation. On December 2, he asked the Secretaries of War and Navy together with the Petroleum Administrator for War and the WPB Chairman to meet to decide on Canol. A week later, three of the members agreed that the project should be dropped at a saving of $30 million, but War Secretary Stimson disagreed and said the savings would only be $10 million.

In responding to the Committee's inquiry, the Army decided the best strategy would be to assert that Canol was a great success. On November 10, 1943, Somervell had instructed one of his minions how to handle the Truman Committee if it blasted Canol: "You should be ready with our public relations outfit to put our best foot forward so that we will not be hurt by the blast and, on the contrary, so that we can be helped. It seems to me that our best line is that if we had the thing to do over again, we would double the size of the installation."[287]

At the start of the hearings, Patterson stated that the Army was "assured" of 20,000 barrels a day from a pool of 50 to 100 million barrels. These amounts were never to be achieved nor could a four-inch line have transported that much oil. Under tough questioning, Patterson reminded the Committee that the Joint Chiefs had found the project to be necessary. Then followed an exchange destined to be famous in the annals of the Committee:

Mr. Patterson. What are you laughing at, Mr Fulton?

Mr. Fulton [Committee counsel]. No matter.

Mr. Patterson. You have been laughing all through this. I haven't seen the humor in it yet.

Mr. Fulton. I have been laughing at the concept that any supply, no matter what is was, would be valuable, without regard to the cost in man-hours and materials together. [288]

Patterson might later regret his testimony, because Fulton would write the Truman Committee report later that month and, in 1945, Patterson, a former judge, would be denied a coveted Supreme Court appointment by President Truman.

Graham had a disastrous and embarrassing appearance before the Committee, repeatedly stating that he was not concerned about cost. He himself was a dollar-a-year man, the ilk that Truman disliked. Ickes had quipped that Graham "was worth every penny of it."

On December 20, 1942, it was Somervell's turn. He arrived with a retinue of four brigadier generals and several other officers. For four and a half hours, Fulton and Senator Harley Kilgore, a West Virginia Democrat, subjected him to the kind of rigorous questioning that he had never suffered previously. He could not respond to some questions, because he lacked precise information. When asked why the War Department had not prepared data for his presentation, he said that he did not need to prepare an alibi. He kept up the prevarication. He claimed that by recycling an existing refinery, "no extra steel was used." When Senator Kilgore pressed him, he admitted that perhaps a 1,000 tons had been used. Kilgore asked for an accurate report, and Somervell sent the Committee data showing that 7,787 tons of new steel was used in the refinery, more than enough to build a tanker with a 128,000 barrel capacity. He continued to justify his failure to consult other agencies, because Canol was essentially none of their business.

Somervell was forced to admit that the pipeline was not complete and probably would not be ready before May 1944. He reported that oil from Norman Wells was being pumped into the pipe, although it could not yet be pumped to Whitehorse, because hundreds of miles of pipe remained to be laid. Fulton suggested that the oil would simply be pumped back and forth until May. Apparently, putting oil in the pipe, like the push to complete the Canol service road by the end of December 1943, were part of an effort to show some progress before the Truman Committee issued its report.

Finally, Somervell was reduced to citing the Joint Chiefs's decision and the "military necessity" defense. But he admitted that, if he had known at the outset that the project would not be completed until 1944, he probably would not have ordered it. By this admission, he abandoned the "best line," that Canol capacity should be doubled, urged on his aide only a month earlier. Truman, known as a generous chairman, let others do almost all of the questioning, limiting himself to pointing out that the Navy had not been consulted. Somervell could only refer to the Joint Chiefs once again, and Truman gaveled the hearings to a close.

Later that month as the Truman Committee report was being written, Roosevelt responded to a question about Canol. The White House summary reported:

> The President was asked whether he had been aware of the ultimate cost of the Canol pipeline project when he had given his approval of the undertaking. Mr. Roosevelt replied that at the time, he had given approval without regard to the possible cost, in the

belief that the development of additional oil-produc-
ing areas in Canada were of the utmost importance
to the defense of the Northwest.[289]

In fact, it was not clear that Roosevelt had ever "given
his approval"[290] to Canol, as distinct from the Alcan Highway, but the Canol decision was undoubtedly made without
any consideration of cost. His press statement was a much
needed boost to Somervell.

On January 8, 1944, the Truman Committee released its
report on Canol. It was a ringing condemnation, obviously
unaffected by Roosevelt's defense. There had been no
study; there was no cost estimate or limit; alternatives had
not been considered; the target date was unrealistic; the
project sopped up needed resources. But the most serious
charge was that Somervell had persisted in his error even
when new information became available: "There may be
some slight excuse for General Somervell's original hasty
decision in view of the tremendous pressure on him at the
time, but his continued insistence on the project in the face
of these repeated warnings is inexcusable."[291]

The Committee also criticized the agreements with the
Canadian Government and Imperial Oil, but blamed Somervell: "There is no indication that Canada would have
refused to discuss fully the equities of the situation or that it
would not have been possible to have obtained a more equitable contract from Canada."[292] The Committee found that
neither Canada nor Imperial were "greedy and sought to
take advantage of the United States."[293] In effect, the Committee said to the War Department: If Canol is as bad as we
think it is, you should have dropped it, but if Canol is as
good as you claim it is, you should not have given it away to
the Canadians.

The Committee's conclusion was stated in italics: "*The
committee is definitely of the opinion that the Canol project
should not have been undertaken, and that it should have
been abandoned when the difficulties were called to the
attention of the War Department.*"[294] It did not recommend
termination, because the project was so far along and left

the decision to the War Department. Almost at the end of its report, the Committee criticized the Alcan Highway itself, saying that if the project were reviewed from its inception, it might not have been found any more necessary than Canol. "It is noteworthy that the material for the construction of the airports, and to a large extent for the highway itself, was transported without use of the highway, and that the airports were completed and in use before the highway was finished,"[295] the report concluded.

Despite the stinging rebuke contained in report, which Connally and Senator Carl Hatch of New Mexico, both Democrats, tried to soften somewhat by a separate statement, Somervell's career did not suffer. When the report was issued, Patterson issued a statement that "the War department has complete confidence in the ability, judgment and performance of General Somervell."[296] He got his fourth star, although his supposed ambition of succeeding General Marshall was not realized. But he had caused Roosevelt political embarrassment and been forced to call upon his superiors to protect his decision. And he had helped Truman make Canol, which one of Somervell's aides called "one fly speck,"[297] into a major war story, far eclipsing the Alcan Highway.

Somervell retired just after the end of the War and became President of Koppers Company, Inc., then a major coke concern. In 1948, he addressed the Industrial College of the Army Forces and told the budding logisticians: "Congress is the board of directors of the Armed Forces. Like businessmen, you must keep your board of directors informed and sympathetic to your needs."[298] The official historian of the Armed Services Forces, an adulatory apologist for Somervell, was forced a few years later to admit that Somervell had not followed his suggestion himself, saying that his attitude did not "make for harmonious legislative relations" and that criticism of him "may have had some justification...."[299]

The report did not put an end to Canol. In June 1944, Patterson asked for and received a $16.4 million appropriation to complete and operate it. Members of the Truman Committee only briefly opposed this appropriation, recognizing that Congress was unlikely to deny the Joint Chiefs of Staff any spending they requested, especially so late in the project.

But the Committee expected to find out the reason for the Joint Chiefs' support of Canol when the war ended. So the Committee's Canol investigation continued. Fulton asked the War Department for an estimate of the cost of supplying from other sources the same fuel as was covered by the new appropriation. Using Lower 48 sources and shipping through Skagway, the Army determined, without apparent embarrassment, that the job could be done for $2.6 million. Fulton also found that shipping was available. The Army had apparently thought the investigation would end, but in July Fulton told Somervell's aide that it would not be dropped:

> Well, I know that Kilgore and Truman on the Democratic side and Ferguson on the Republican side will never let this drop and they intend at some point particularly to show one project from start to finish and particularly to show the way in which, in effect, huge sums of money, available materials and so on, in their opinion, just deliberately wasted to protect the name of a man who has made a mistake and wasn't big enough to admit it.[300]

The next time the Committee considered Canol was late 1946. It asked Admiral Ernest J. King, a member of the Joint Chiefs, to provide the basis for the October 1943 decision to persist with Canol. He refused to provide any more detail, restating the position that Canol was a military necessity for reasons that were not revealed. In October 1946, the Committee issued a new report critical of Somervell and King. The Admiral objected, stating that he should not be held individually responsible for a decision of the Joint Chiefs.

A new public hearing resulted from the spat, but this time the Committee was given the Joint Chiefs' declassified file. In his testimony, King insisted that the Joint Chiefs had merely approved a recommendation of the Joint Production Survey Committee, the body charged with identifying war materiel needs. He resorted to the traditional claims that Canol was needed for national security, still an effective way of cutting off outside questioning. Admittedly, by early 1945, the Joint Chiefs had concluded that it had no value as part of the nation's permanent defense.

Just after the hearing, an entirely new reason for persisting with Canol had been offered by "an informed source" who had seen the files of the Joint Production Survey Committee.[301] While Canol was originally intended to supply fuel to the Alcan system, it produced disappointing results and was replaced by the Pacific route. But the project was continued, the story went, to mislead the Japanese into believing that the northern supply was still valuable, causing them to keep forces assigned to the Alaska sector, while the Americans advanced further south in the Pacific. The final $29 million was not meant to produce oil; it was a ploy.

Fulton had been wrong about Truman's future interest in Canol. While King and the Committee wrangled, Truman was asked if Admiral King should be directed by him to disclose the Joint Chief's thinking on Canol. President Truman said that there was no point in investigating beyond the initial report. "[T]he Canol project is a dead horse," he said. "Those investigations and reports were made for the purpose of preventing the digging up of dead horses."[302] Truman thought there was no point in King testifying. King, who by that time had testified, declined to comment on the story.

The New York Times reported the new revelation as if it explained everything, both King's reluctance to testify and Truman's saying that his investigation had been sufficient, when, in fact, he could not have been aware of the plan to fool the enemy.[303] Eventually the official history of Somervell's command tepidly accepted the explanation that Canol kept the Japanese worried about an attack from the North.[304]

The strategic ploy story does not withstand serious scrutiny. The Truman Committee hearings were public and so was its January 1944 report. The Japanese could easily have found out that the project was delayed and the amount of fuel that it would deliver through a four-inch line would be tiny. Troops were openly being withdrawn from Alaska when the Joint Chiefs made their Canol decision, hardly consistent with the alleged plan to fool the enemy. Because neither King nor the Joint Chiefs minutes even hinted at this strategy, it seems likely that the official history of the Army Service Forces, commanded by Somervell, was meant mainly to indemnify its leader from a negative judgment of history.

The hearings and the January 1944 report has been critical of the Army for offering the Canadians a sweetheart deal and Imperial Oil a bonanza. Canada agreed to allow oil prospecting and the construction of the pipeline and refinery. At the end of the war, the oil rights would revert to Canada, which could purchase the physical facilities at their commercial value. Without asking for it, Canada had been given the similar rights to the Canol project as it had obtained for the Alaska Highway. Meanwhile, the Army's contractors would prospect on Imperial oil leases at U.S. expense. Imperial would sell the crude to the Army at exorbitant prices, although some of the proceeds would be held in reserve to fund an Imperial purchase of American-financed physical facilities. These agreements had been put in place rapidly to quell any Canadian objections either to the project or to the fact that Canol, a project entirely on Canadian territory at the outset, had been approved by the Americans before the Canadians knew anything about it.

The Army took the Truman Committee criticism to heart and sought to renegotiate the deals with Canada and Imperial. Hugh Keenleyside, on behalf of the Canadian External Affairs Ministry, understood American intentions, reporting that: "the interpretation of misinterpretation of the principles underlying Lease-Lend, have led to a popular feeling in the United States that the Administration will be failing in its duty if it does not now provide for the acquisition of post-war profit from the wartime expenditure in foreign countries."[305] The American presence raised the possibility that it would stay as an integral and controlling element in the Canadian economy, in the West at least, even after the War. The Canadians were coming to dislike the idea of the United States owning facilities in their country. They wanted to get rid of any American ownership rights at the same time as the Army wanted to get a better commercial deal for the oil. The answer seemed simple: Canada should purchase from the United States any permanent facility that the Americans had built in its territory. Fortunately for Canada, it was building large U.S. dollar reserves, thanks to military spending north of the border. The Canadians were given their chance to renegotiate agreements on Northwest facilities, when the Army itself, under Truman's prodding, asked for contract revisions.

Canada embarked on its policy of buying out the Americans, just as the public hearings in Canol began. Its first move was to obtain the NWSR airfields. Then, with the principal of the buy-out established, they began negotiating with the Americans on Canol in December 1943. They immediately rejected any claim to a right to a return on investment, as Canol was a defense project not a commercial undertaking. Canada would not allow the Americans to make a profit on the facilities, simply to get their commercial value. This firm rejection of American claims effectively ended American post-war ownership claims. Because the United States had so irresponsibly lavished funds on Canol construction, it could never hope to get its investment back, much less a return.

By the time the negotiations turned to Imperial, the Americans wanted the best economic deal they could get and no further involvement. The deal would result in all American physical assets being transferred to Imperial after the war. In the meantime, with a reduced royalty payout authorized by the Canadian Government, Imperial would cut its prices to the Americans. But the Canadian Government also said that it had the right to seize the property, reflecting its concern that Imperial was, after all, really an American company. Under a decision of the PJBD, the United States was given the right to keep the Canol facilities for as much as a year after the War. Ultimately, Canada had ended any threat of American ownership or control. On the American side, *The New York Times* trumpeted the price cuts as a victory.[306] The report assumed that there would be oil to buy at the lower price. But six months earlier, it had reported that "if the project is abandoned by the United States there will be no justification for its continuance by Canada on the present scale [thus allowing the oilfield to revert to pre-Canol status]".[307]

The deal would never have to be completely implemented. The United States wanted out of Canol even before the War ended; the fuel was simply too expensive. The Canadians, willing to allow the appraisal of the property to take place promptly, made it clear that no matter what the price, it would not purchase the Canol facilities. The Americans did not like this decision, but Canada had always estimated the northern reserves well below the U.S. projections. The implication of the U.S. position was that Canada should purchase the refinery and the pipeline, but let them stand idle. The Canadians would not accept any suggestion that the United States could retain ownership. Canol was dead. In 1947, Imperial would purchase the refinery for use in Alberta for $1 million. American firms paid $700,000 for the pipeline, used as scrap.

These revenues were small compensation for the costs of Canol. The price tag was a result of the haste with which the decision was made, but also because of the imbedded belief that a quick response depends on the ability to exceed budgetary constraints. Deals were quickly made with large contractors to construct projects such as Canol without concern for the allocation of public resources, deemed to be virtually limitless, nor for the profits gained by companies that worked under cost-plus rules.

The Truman Committee avoided any discussion of the contracts or contractors, simply commenting on the huge cost of the pipeline and refinery compared with projects in the Lower 48. Bechtel was never called as a witness, but believed that he was doing just what Somervell asked of him. His companies, three of which worked on Canol,

"profited handsomely" from the cost-plus contract.[308] Some
of the costs were the exorbitant equipment rentals, which
radio commentator Fulton Lewis, Jr., said yielded 40 percent margins. Gaining splashy headlines, Wyoming Republican Senator Edward V. Robertson called for an
investigation, but nothing came of his complaint.

A similar fate befell an even more serious threat to
Bechtel. In April 1944, criminal conspiracy charges were
lodged in Fairbanks against the Bechtel and Callahan companies for the markup of items used in construction priced
in excess of normal retail prices. False claims for reimburse-
ment were alleged in the indictment. The Office of Price
Administration had previously filed civil actions against the
firms.[309] Bechtel emerged unscathed and remained a favored
government contractor, staffed by top government retirees.

The only other obvious winner from the Canol project
was Senator Truman. He was careful, even while the Committee was on the attack, to give its targets a chance to pull
back. For example, the Canol Report said that, when Patterson had testified glowingly about Canol, he might not have
been aware of all of the facts uncovered by the Committee.
But Patterson did not take the chance to retreat. Truman let
others carry the burden of much of the hostile questioning,
while he gained fame for staging the event. Most significantly, in attempting to avoid the mistakes of the Civil
War's Committee on the Conduct of the War, he had faith-
fully demurred whenever strategic requirements were cited
as the reason for the Army's actions. At Stimson's request,
he kept the Committee away from the Manhattan Engineering District, the cover for the development of the atomic
bomb, a project under Somervell's supervision. All the
while, he accomplished his original mission of getting
defense contracts more widely distributed.

Truman had always supported Roosevelt's policies, both
during the pre-war New Deal era and during the war. But he
was having his own impact, as one analyst noted: "Truman's unsettling discoveries went on and on, his reports of
waste and corruption, lavishly covered in the press, making
upsetting reading for Roosevelt."[310] Having gained national

stature for his independence, his endorsement of Roosevelt's war management was valuable to the President, a major switch from an earlier time when Truman needed White House support. Because of the war, Truman had no reluctance in supporting an unprecedented fourth term for Roosevelt, although he had opposed the third.

Some Republicans thought his support for the President, coming right after the two had clashed on Canol, undermined the reputation he had built for keeping the Committee out of partisan politics. But he seemed not to suffer from any retaliation. Michigan G.O.P. Senator Arthur H. Vandenburg, an ardent critic of the Democratic Administration, was pleased to get Truman to admit Roosevelt's failings in putting together an effective supply system, the second time that he acknowledged Truman's objectivity. [311] As President, Truman would be able to launch a strong, bipartisan foreign policy, thanks almost exclusively to the unswerving and surprising support of Senator Vandenburg.

Ultimately, the Democratic party bosses succeeded in pressuring Roosevelt to accept Truman as his running mate as a way of keeping the New Deal coalition together. Vice President Wallace was liberal enough for the North and too liberal for the South. Truman of Missouri was almost a Southerner, but his strong stands on civil rights made him even more popular than Roosevelt with many Northern black voters. Thanks to the Committee and Canol, the last major investigation just winding up as the election year began, in just over three years the obscure Mr. Truman had become a popular national figure. That the bosses picked him was a tribute not only to his popularity but also to his skill, for they knew that sometime in the next four years, he would be president.

PART V. CONSEQUENCES

CHAPTER 11.

THE U.S. ARMY OF OCCUPATION

One story that has become so much a part of Alcan lore that it cannot be verified as true recounted that telephone operators at U.S. headquarters in Edmonton were said occasionally to answer the phone, "Army of Occupation." The story went that one caller was a distinctly unhappy Canadian general. Whether or not the story is true, the American presence in Northwest Canada took on the character of an invasion, and the degree of U.S. control was more like the occupation of a defeated country than cooperation with an ally.

Whenever military personnel of one country are stationed on the territory of another, the two countries often arrive at an agreement on the "status of forces," a way of determining who will have jurisdiction over illegal acts of the visiting troops. Usually, the foreign government wants and gets, at a minimum, an accord providing that its personnel remain subject to its jurisdiction for military infractions. With Canada, matters became much more complicated.

The American presence consisted of both military and civilian personnel. Because the PRA and other contractors were actually working for the Corps of Engineers, they were subject to U.S. military law. Many Canadians also worked on Alcan projects for private contractors. Would they be under the U.S. or Canadian legal systems? Finally, both American and Canadian civilians, having no connection with the Alcan projects, were in the area where the construction and military operations were taking place. Who had jurisdiction over them?

Before Alcan, the Canadian Northwest was only lightly policed. In 1940, the Royal Canadian Mounted Police had 20 Mounties in the Yukon, more than half of them based in Dawson City, then the capital of the territory and well off the Alcan Highway route. In Whitehorse, where thousands of Americans would soon arrive, there were only three. More significantly, there were still only three Mounties there in 1942 climbing to seven in 1943.[312] This thin force reflected both the somewhat detached attitude of Ottawa to the Northwest and the relatively small population of Canada, then making a large contribution to Allied forces in Europe.

The RCMP was soon supplemented by at least three groups of military police: The Army MPs, the RCAF provost marshal and the Army Air Corps police. In all of the PJBD meetings and in diplomatic exchanges between the two governments, nobody had thought to discuss the jurisdictional authority of these units. Unilaterally, the Canadian Government gave the U.S. military police the right to deal with all charges against American personnel, except murder, manslaughter and rape. But the Canadians did not give up their right to try lesser offenses as well.

The Americans then began a long and persistent effort to gain an ever-increasing amount of legal jurisdiction in the areas where they were working. First, in December 1942, they demanded "exclusive and unlimited criminal jurisdiction" over offenses, including those by Americans against Canadians, and offered Canada reciprocity. The Canadian Government rejected the request, despite statements by the U.S. State Department that Britain had agreed and that the only country hosting America troops that was offered reciprocity was Canada. Before the Canadians could reconsider their position, the United States withdrew the offer of reciprocity on the grounds that the U.S. Constitution did not permit it.[313] Because Britain was ready to give the United States the authority it requested, the Canadians gave way in March 1943. They retained concurrent jurisdiction on the three major crimes.

Sharing the right to prosecute caused problems. Both Alberta and British Columbia, enjoying more independence under the Canadian confederation than was the case for American states, were nettled that they had been stripped of their jurisdiction. But the problems went beyond mere matters of pride. Procedures and punishments differed between the Canadians and Americans. For example, rape could be punished by death under U.S. military law, but only by ten years in prison under Alberta law. To avoid double jeopardy, a person could only be tried in one jurisdiction.[314]

A still bigger issue was the use of the American military legal system to protect American soldiers from harsh Canadian sentences. In some cases, Americans were simply removed from Canada to avoid local jurisdiction and in others, they were given more lenient sentences than they would have received at the hands of Canadian justice. The Canadians remained unhappy. An April 1943 memorandum in the Northwest Service Command files noted that "relationships between the United States and Canada are being seriously embarrassed by reasons of sex crimes committed by United States troops against Canadian women."[315]

The Americans kept up the pressure and finally in December 1943, the Canadians gave them all they had demanded. The United States gained exclusive jurisdiction over American and Canadian personnel working for it for any offense. Once a detainee was requested by American officials, the Canadian authorities were required to turn the person over to the Americans. In practice, however, the Americans occasionally let the Canadians try alleged offenders under their own system. By October 1944, the American law had been amended to offer a small degree of reciprocity by allowing Canadian military courts in the United States to try Canadian military personnel stationed there.[316]

While the formal outcome was all that the United States had sought, it rankled in Canada. From the outset, local people had been discontent with the ability of the U.S. military to try cases where Canadians were the victims. This kind of immunity, characteristic of rights given to friendly forces on foreign territory, never builds good relations.[317] But the problem went even further as the Canadians encountered arrogant behavior by American military police who were not reluctant to leave the impression that they ran the Canadian Northwest. Even Canadian law enforcement personnel were treated by the Americans as if they had no authority and could be pushed around at will. In one July 1943 incident, three Canadian police officers in uniform were stopped by American MPs for speeding and told to turn themselves in, which they did not do.[318]

Local civilians found themselves arrested and beaten for offenses purely civil in nature and having nothing to do with U.S. military activities. Hearing of one case in Whitehorse where MPs had injured women riding in a car and threatened to shoot the men, George Black, the voluble Yukon member of Canadian Parliament, called the MPs, the "U.S. Army Gestapo,"[319] strong words at the time. Such events and the local reactions to them increasingly fed the sentiment that the Americans were an occupation force of the kind imposed on enemies but not on friends.

Yet there was broad cooperation among the several law enforcement entities. Despite the omnipresence of the MPs, most Canadians had little contact with law enforcement. Until the American troops finally departed in 1946, the odd jurisdictional structure remained in place. Like many other aspects of the Alcan projects, Canada would put up with much during the war, but would remember the lessons well afterwards and would not again allow Americans to gain such a foothold.

If the impact of law enforcement issues on the Canadian Northwest was direct and obvious, the effect of the Alcan projects on the native population was more profound and longer-lasting. Jurisdiction could be restored after the war, but a way of life and life itself could not.

The Canadian Northwest was sparsely populated with only 4,900 people in the Yukon. Many, possibly a majority, of the people were natives, descendants of those who had crossed the land bridge from Asia in the prehistoric past. While they might have appeared primitive to white people, they were not, living a stable existence adapted to the difficult terrain and cold climate. They had previously been in contact with white people and some had become Christians. The fur trade, an important part of their economy, had also put them in direct contact with outsiders and the money economy. In addition to the whites running trading posts and missionaries, the natives came into contact with Mounties and Government officials. Despite these contacts, their way of life was not corrupted or radically changed by contact with whites. They were nomadic, their small communities traveling with the season to harvest the fruits of the forests and streams. They had not journeyed far from the traditional hunter-gatherer life.[320]

Beside this permanent portion of the Northwest community were whites, many of them the remnants of the thousands who had trekked north during the Klondike Gold Rush around the turn of the Twentieth Century. These people were responsible for the infrastructure that had been created since then: the railway, the towns and the stern wheelers. But these people did not usually stay in the Northwest, just as many back-to-the-earth people, decades later, would abandon their fantasies. Life on the Alaska side of the border was much the same.

The Canadian Government, with limited resources, a small population and a huge territory was content to leave this society alone, and people there had little contact with the rest of Canadian society and political life. The Alcan projects changed life in the bush at a pace unlike any previous event, even the Gold Rush. Despite rumors about the new road, native communities were stunned when their camps were suddenly forced to scuttle before the enormous Cats, which had materialized literally out of nowhere.

The Americans seemed to see natives as either part of the scenery or sometimes as useful guides and helpers. Little respect was shown for their culture, although they were able to turn their culture into commerce by selling many handmade souvenirs to soldiers. Until native towns were put off limits to the military, native women were regarded as available for sexual exploitation. Natives found themselves the object of the same kind of racial discrimination as they saw the black soldiers experience.[321]

Some found work. Perhaps most importantly, they helped guide the surveyors laying out the route for the pioneer road and, later, for the Canol Road. They knew the land in their local area and could lay out a path for the road faster than could any other method. They also worked handling freight and in these tasks did work much like that done by some of the black soldiers. But almost none got permanent, good-paying work for their efforts.

Some lost work. As land was put into parks and preserves to prevent the American soldiers, hunting in their spare time, from decimating the last of the game, the natives were deprived of traditional hunting and trapping grounds. Even where the Government finally conceded that they could continue to trap, they then needed licenses for specific areas, and intra-family disputes over these license rights came to replace traditional informal arrangements that had worked satisfactorily for generations. And the game began to move away from the route of the highway, areas where it had once been plentiful.

Inevitably natives began to be drawn to the road, which would later come to be called "the gravel magnet."[322] They came because they could no longer earn their livelihood in the bush and because they could earn cash on the road or in the towns. The changes wrought by the Alcan Highway would prevent them ever from returning to the land. While these changes were gradual and also reflected the declining fur trade, they were inevitable.

The greatest impact of the road on native life came as an aftershock. Long ignored, perhaps because they wanted it that way, the natives had led their lives far removed from the public policies of Canada. But the Alaska Highway had made Ottawa more conscious of the Northwest, its people and their needs. The opening of this remote corner of

Canada brought with it the requirement for a more active government role in its life.

As the war came to an end, Canada adopted a Family Allowance Act, which mandated assistance to natives on the same basis as support given to non-natives. Paternalism remained, as benefits were distributed in kind not in the cash payments to non-natives. Benefits were used to attract young natives into schools, which had the inevitable effect of drawing their families to the communities along the road: the "gravel magnet" began operating at full strength. By 1945, assistance to natives was placed under a new Ministry of National Health and Welfare instead of being incidental to other Government activities in the Northwest.[323] Canada was moving to institute social welfare programs similar to those in European countries, but the natives might well have been ignored by these initiatives had not the Alcan Highway created the infrastructure enabling the Government to deliver social services. However admirable their goals, the Alcan complex and the newly available social programs destroyed the old way of life. Natives, remembering their free and nomadic lives, lamented the society of dependency and lost wilderness skills in which their children came to live.[324]

When Washington had demanded and Ottawa had acquiesced in the development of the Alcan projects, nobody considered the effect that such sudden and enormous infrastructure endeavors would have on the society it would crush. Just as the conquest of the American West by the U.S. Army had turned proud Native Americans into Government dependents, that same U.S. Army, no less heedless than it had been 70 years earlier, had created a new class of dependents.

More direct and even more devastating was the effect of the American presence on native health. Unknowingly, the Americans brought with them an array of common illnesses, which were disastrous to the isolated native communities that had not built up immunities to them. In the community of Teslin for example, in less than a year, the people had been hit with outbreaks of measles, dysentery, jaundice, whooping cough, mumps and meningitis.[325] While white communities might experience such illnesses in small parts of the population and with few fatalities, the death toll in Teslin and other communities like it rose to include the scores of people, a large part of the population. At Teslin, 95 percent of the population had measles. In Lower Post, 15 people out of 150 died.[326] Diphtheria broke out along the Canol Road. The natives would long remember the winter of 1942-43 in which many families lost members to the diseases that came with the soldiers. Official health statistics would show that in those two years, the natural growth in the native population in the Yukon reversed with deaths exceeding births by as much as 42 per cent. It took four more years before it would return to its normal growth rate.[327]

The Americans also brought with them alcohol, which had been carefully regulated by the Canadian Government and denied to the natives. An illegal trade had existed before the War, but exploded with the coming of the U.S. Army. Providing alcohol to natives was severely punished under Canadian law, but given the pervasiveness of the beer and liquor available to the soldiers, that law was difficult to enforce. Its illegal status drove the price up, and frequently the natives were asked to pay with sexual favors. The natives usually had little trouble with law enforcement agencies, but the sudden growth in native convictions, beginning in 1942, could be directly tied to their increased use of alcohol.[328]

Although the Alcan invasion brought native health disastrously into modern times, the Army reacted with something more than its usual indifference. Army Medical Corps doctors spread out to the settlements, caring for the natives and providing medications and supplies. At first, the Yukon Government tried to stop American doctors from practicing, but soon retreated. The quality and timeliness of Canadian health care, provided through the RCMP, was poor. American help was prompt and reasonably effective, though not entirely altruistic, as the American doctors tried, successfully, to keep the spread of the waves of epidemics from reaching soldiers and contractors' employees.

The Alcan forces not only changed the lives of the people living on the land, they changed the land itself. Construction had a necessarily harmful effect. The Americans had been given an unlimited right to cut timber and used the logs for heating and road building. Despite Canadian appeals for the Americans to observe conservation principles by selective cutting and the use of buffers to protect scenic views, the land was being stripped bare of timber, which in that cold climate, would take decades to recover. American demand for wood, accompanied by waste when thousands of cords remained unused, forced Canadian conservationists into rearguard actions to salvage some stands until the war was over.

The other inevitable loss came to the permafrost, with which the Americans were completely unfamiliar. The permafrost supplied stability to the land, and once its cover had been removed and it began to melt, it would take many years to recover. In the meantime, its absence would only make construction slower and more difficult, and the measures taken to deal with the problem would only make matters worse, as more brush and trees had to be cut to provide new cover.

Another unfortunate by-product of the construction were forest fires. Inflammable materials and flame-producing equipment set off blazes during construction, but the most important source were cigarettes thrown off the road into piles of slash and other combustibles. The troops seemed to think the forest was endless and, in any case, that fire prevention was somebody else's worry. In one of the rare cases in which Canada vigorously protested the Army's actions, the military issued tough orders to bring the blazes, some of which had been enormous, down to a more reasonable level.

Perhaps the greatest environmental impact was on wildlife. Although stories that just about every other soldier was an experienced hunter were greatly exaggerated, the soldiers, able to obtain resident hunting licenses with relative ease, took a heavy toll of the game. The natives reported a sharp decline in the available wildlife. By September 1942, only six months after the arrival of the first Americans, Canada moved to protect the southwest portion of the Yukon. At the request of its highest ranking federal official in the area, the Government moved swiftly to create the Kluane game preserve.[329] Whatever the truth about the extent of the soldiers' depredations, and there was much debate about the degree of harm they had done, they did change the face of hunting in a significant part of the Yukon. The game preserve became the Kluane National Park, one of the most stunningly beautiful park areas on the North American continent, and hunting would never again be allowed there. In an unexpected way, the American invasion had created a Canadian national treasure.

Of course, the opening of the Canadian Northwest by the Alaska Highway threatened to encourage more development. But the area remained remote in the minds of prospective tourists and while tourists' vehicles ultimately became the prevalent users of long stretches of the road, much of the land was able to heal.

All of these incursions into the traditional Canadian system represented assaults, big and small, on Canadian sovereignty over its own territory. Taken together and added to the actual construction work, they were a real but as yet unrecognized threat to the territorial integrity of Canada and the survival of its control over the Northwest.

Despite the Canadian military's belief that the Alcan Highway was unnecessary, Prime Minister Mackenzie King had agreed to the U.S. request to build the road. But he remained worried about American intentions. He had been warned by Norman Robertson, the day-to-day head of the Department of External Affairs, that the United States showed an increasing inclination "to regard Canada as an internal domestic relationship rather than an international one."[330] Another official reported that the United States had begun "to order Canada around."[331]

This realization came almost as soon as the United States entered the war. As a neutral, it had shown some deference to Canada; as a superpower, which recognized that Canada itself did not have sufficient resources to defend the north portion of the continent, it wanted mutual, but not equal, cooperation. In fact, the United States went so far as to ask that the part of the Canadian Navy based on the Canadian West Coast, be placed under its command. Canada refused.

The issues for Canada were clear, and they had to be handled in a pragmatic way. It was increasingly resentful of Britain assuming that it could act on behalf of Canada, as a member of the Commonwealth. Mackenzie King saw the Commonwealth as an organization of equals, and he may have been more aware than even Churchill himself that, in the postwar world, Britain would not have the wealth and power to dominate its former colonies. The United States, the emergent superpower and its North American neighbor, was both a natural counterbalance to Great Britain and an essential ally in defending Canada's own national territory. Yet he was clearly worried about the United States turning out to be too much of a good thing. Mackenzie King would have to proceed carefully and, true to form, he would almost always keep his thoughts to himself.

From the outset, the Americans moved in as if they had the right to do so, even when the Canadian Government had not yet agreed. Work on the Alcan Highway actually began before the official exchange of notes constituting the agreement between the two governments. These developments were characteristic of the institutional problems, which would continue to cause uneasiness in Ottawa. The Canadian Government dealt with the United States through the America Legation, not yet an Embassy, in Ottawa and the State Department. U.S. diplomats were careful to respect Canadian rights. But it became clear that the War Department paid scant attention to the role played by diplomats and believed it could act with great latitude. When confronted, the War Department would resort to claiming that there had been some misunderstanding and that it had thought it had been given blanket authority to carry out a project however it chose.

One way the War Department could override Canadian objections was to keep increasing the size of a proposed project to the point where it exceeded Canadian capacity to finance or control it, leaving the American Army to do what it wanted. The Canadian response was to jointly manage facilities in areas where personnel came in contact with Canadian civilians and let the Americans have free rein in more remote areas.

Especially worrisome were America claims that the U.S. investment in wartime facilities gave it rights in Canada that would outlast the war. In January 1943, Mayor LaGuardia, as U.S. chairman of the PJBD, said that "of course American planes would be able after the war to use the bases in Canada which are being built by American money."[332] American post-war intentions were confirmed by information Mackenzie King received from Vincent Massey, the chief Canadian diplomat in London.[333] Later in 1943, the Americans would propose to rename the road so that it would be called the "Alaska Highway." Canada agreed, but Mackenzie King insisted the name change not be adopted by Congress, so that the Americans would not take upon themselves the right to name roads in Canada with concurrent post-war rights to their use. The Canadian Government once again explicitly rejected a request by the U.S. Government to revise the original agreement to allow for post-war use.

Canol was more of the same. Canadian officials did not think the project was worth the effort, but were willing to allow it so long as the effort was American and the postwar benefit, if any, was Canadian. Once again, the Army proceeded to roll across the territory as if they were at home. The line of airfields on the Canol supply route, some parts of the pipeline and many feeder roads were simply started without approval, which sometimes came later. The sole Canadian patrol vessel in the Arctic Islands had simply been

seized by the United States to transport supplies and personnel for two new weather stations. The Canadians only found
out about the boat when a Canadian inspector visited the
area.[334] From the Canadian perspective, one later commentator concluded: "Regardless of their reasons, in 1942 many
Americans in the field assumed they had the same powers
as a military occupation."[335]

This situation was inherently unstable. If Canada did
nothing, the United States would continue, intentionally or
not, to control the Northwest and tie it economically to the
United States. While recognizing the common sense of a
closer relationship between the United States and Canada,
Britain was not willing to see its own role and influence
obliterated without a fight. The British concern turned the
tide.

The British diplomatic representative in Ottawa was
Malcolm MacDonald, who been a British cabinet minister,
but had taken a demotion to Canada because of its growing
importance and his personal relationship with Mackenzie
King. MacDonald, the son of a British Prime Minister, had
become acquainted with the Canadian leader during his official visits to London. Once in Canada, he was approached
by people from the Canadian North, undoubtedly strong
British loyalists, who told him of American activities on the
three Alcan projects. They complained of the freedom with
which the Americans acted.

MacDonald took two trips to the Northwest to see for
himself. His second trip in March 1943 galvanized him into
action. On his return to Ottawa, he prepared an unusual document stating his views and met with Mackenzie King. His
message was deemed so important that he was invited to
meet with the Canadian War Cabinet. He formalized the
document and sent it to Clement Atlee, the future British
Prime Minister then in charge of the Dominions Office.

MacDonald's "Note on Developments in North-Western
Canada"[336] praised Canada for its policy in the Northwest,
but found that "Canadian authorities have too little influence on the shaping of these important affairs in Canadian

territory." He warned that "the American authorities have gained increasing control of what is done, how it is done and where it is done...", and noted the problem of dealing with the State Department, which had been ignored by the U.S. Army.

He documented American abuses. He reported that the Americans were taking aerial photos at will, perhaps in anticipation of future development plans.

According to MacDonald's informants, the purposes for all of the unchecked activity by U.S. personnel were, first, laying the groundwork for American commercial aviation in the post-war period and, second, preparing for war with the Soviet Union. At the same time, commercial interests then involved in construction, like Bechtel, could be expected to stir up "unpleasant agitation in Congress" to induce the Roosevelt administration to force revision of the agreements giving Canada exclusive rights in the area after the war. Add to all of these pressures the sentiments "of those Western Canadians who are inclined to assert that the West receives little sympathy and help from Eastern Canada, and that its destiny lies in incorporation with the United States of America."

MacDonald contrasted the presence of the Americans and the Canadians in Edmonton. Having built scores of new buildings there, the Americans had placed "a whole Army division in the region." About 13,000 Americans comprised the local force. "The regular Canadian organization in Edmonton on the other hand consists of one man." He turned out to be a part-time employee. Liaison between Ottawa and Washington had once served to control the course of events, but the American field presence was autonomous and did not clear major matters with Washington and certainly not with Ottawa.

After a perfunctory acknowledgment that he could not "claim any real grasp of the problems" and was "not qualified to propose remedies," MacDonald plunged ahead to demonstrate that he both knew more than did the Government in Ottawa and had a solution to propose. He suggested a Canadian organization in Edmonton, composed of representatives of several federal agencies, to be headed by a Commissioner. The headquarters should be "sufficiently imposing to impress everyone with the presence and authority of the Canadian Government." This operation would be responsible for liaison with the Americans and would guard Canadian interests.

MacDonald's cover memo[337] to Atlee was even more blunt. He recognized that his Note might be "impertinent, not to say unconstitutional" for a person acting in the role of an ambassador to send. He told Atlee that the situation was "alarming" and probably worse than he had stated. Finally, he said that he had sent a copy of the Note to Lord Halifax, the British Ambassador to Washington; the Americans did not learn of the Note or its contents. Later that year, MacDonald's book, *Down North*, was published[338], revealing his great affection for the Northwest region, though understating his concerns.

If not unconstitutional, the Note was a most unusual communication between a foreign diplomatic representative and the government to which he was accredited. In itself, it was as much an intervention in Canadian internal affairs as the American invasion on which it reported. The Canadian reaction was divided. Government officials who might find themselves held responsible for the failings which had led to such complete American control did not endorse it, but others agreed with the Note.

At the same time, the Department of External Affairs received a second report, which confirmed what MacDonald had found. Robert Beattie, director of northern research for the Bank of Canada, worried about the size of the U.S. investment and the "ambitions and aggressiveness of the American private airlines" already operating in the Northwest. He issued the sternest warning that "so far as Canada is concerned the Northwest is today in many respects a foreign country." Unless Canada set its own objectives and pursued them, "she will never again regain effective control of the region, nor will she deserve to."[339]

This was no British diplomat showing some restraint; this was an angry Canadian.

Confidential communications were not needed to make the point. Promoters and dreamers were talking publicly about the notion of creating a single economy linking the Canadian and American Northwest regions. Some Canadians believed they had an obligation to push development in the region and would need American involvement, if not U.S. investment, to bring about greater prosperity there. This economy would feed Canadian resources into Washington and Oregon. As early as December 1942, this concept, called CANASKA, was getting front page coverage in an Oregon newspaper.[340] Of course, the wartime projects would help undergird this development. Population could be increased by adding people displaced by the war and other immigrants. The plan looked like it would lead to economic integration, perhaps based on a customs union. All involved in promoting the concept saw Canada as a vacuum that must be filled. Some Americans, who admittedly understood little about Canada or about the Commonwealth, thought that "Britain should hand over Canada in payment of war debts."[341]

Mackenzie King quickly decided to follow the general line of MacDonald's recommendations. The Canadian Government took a series of key actions in quick succession. First, it decided to pay all the costs of airfield construction done by the Americans so that American air carriers would have no basis to claim the right to use the fields after the war. Eventually, Canada purchased permanent facilities along the Alaska Highway, with the total cost amounting to $123.5 million financed out of Canada's mounting U.S. dollar reserves. Just as MacDonald had predicted, the U.S. Congress, in the form of the Truman Committee, had demanded postwar rights in return for its investment, and the demand passed on by the State Department had given Canada a forum to reject firmly any such claims by buying out the investment.

As part of its effort to control the expansion of American efforts to open Canadian airways, the Government refused to allow the Americans to proceed any further in extending its Canol oil field access. While the Americans had to be allowed to keep on with the rapid development of the NWSR, the costs of permanent installations there, too, would be paid by Canada. Not only did it reject U.S. post-war military use of the Alaska Highway, it prevented any change in authority over the airfields. And it began to slow the work of the PJBD rather than quickly agreeing to U.S. requests.

In May 1943, just two months after MacDonald's Note, Mackenzie King appointed Brigadier-General W.W. Forster as "the special commissioner for defence projects in north-west Canada." Forster was given confidential instructions and told that he would report directly to the War Cabinet. Forster was quickly promoted to Major General, probably so that he would outrank the senior American commander in Edmonton.

Forster soon began to supply Ottawa with extensive reports on all areas of Government activity, focusing on the degree to which Canadian intervention was necessary to protect the country's sovereignty. He also took on the task of requiring the Americans to obtain advance authorization for their activities and making sure they followed Canadian laws and regulations. A much more cumbersome, 18-step process for obtaining Canadian approval was put in place, apparently to discourage the Americans from undertaking new projects.

Most importantly Forster sent to Ottawa 41 recommendations on virtually all of the major issues; the road, civil aviation, oil, the environment and, perhaps most importantly, new fire protection regulations.

All of these actions came none too soon. In September 1943, Ray Atherton, the new American ambassador to Canada, told an Ottawa audience that "the best thing for the United States and Alaska is also the best thing for Canada,"[342] and pushed, without much effect, for the extension of the Hyde Park Declaration to the post-war period. Such statements kept the British worried, despite Canada's prompt responses to the MacDonald Note. As late as November 1944, they continued to fear that the Canadians had failed to assert themselves. Sir Patrick Suff, a British official who visited the Northwest, found that the "overwhelming" American presence and the possible peacetime use of seemingly permanent installations "causes a number of officers ... to apprehend the intention on the part of the United States to make the North West Staging Route a Polish Corridor."[343] Between the two World Wars, Poland had owned a strip of territory giving it access to the port of Gdansk, dividing German territory into two parts. Presumably, American intentions would be no more appreciated by Canada, a U.S. ally, than the Polish Corridor had been appreciated by Germany, Poland's once-and-future enemy.

Two major issues overshadowed the discussion of the American presence, one public and the other top secret. Suspicions that the Americans wanted access to Canadian airfields and air space were well founded. The United States was working on a secret plan for a bilateral agreement with Canada, which would give it unfettered use of Canadian air space. In perhaps its first major foreign policy initiative, Canada decided to push for an international organization to regulate civil aviation. The British wanted a Commonwealth-only arrangement to counterbalance the United States. Because the United States did not want to open American air space to others, it was forced to advocate a policy, which would only allow foreign carriers to refuel and fly over, but not to carry passengers or freight. Although Canada won agreement to have an international body adopt regulations, the American insistence on protecting its own air commerce served well for Canada, when the U.S. policy was imported north of the border, and each nation could control the use of its airspace by any other. As with the results of Truman's Canol investigation, the United States was stymied in its Canadian aspirations by its own tactics.

The secret agenda item was uranium. With the Belgian Congo not available as a source, thanks to German control of Belgium, Canada became the world's largest supplier. Both Britain and the United States wanted uranium for their nuclear bomb projects. In 1942, MacDonald had informed Mackenzie King and two close associates of the wartime plans for the bomb and also of the possible peacetime uses. The Canadian Government began to move toward acquiring the one company mining uranium in Canada. Meanwhile, the Americans, while approving British-Canadian cooperation, bought up most of the supply and reneged on their commitment to insure that Britain received what it had requested. The American program had come under the supervision of Maj. Gen. L.R. Groves, who reported to Somervell, the man who had picked him for the job. Groves expected the Canadian and British efforts to be subsidiaries of his Manhattan Project. In any case, Canada believed it was committed under the Hyde Park Declaration to supply the United States and disliked British pressure. By late 1944, the Belgian Congo mine was reopened, and the Canadian uranium issue proved to have a short half-life. A part of the struggle for control of the Canadian Northwest had been about uranium, and Canada won. It had the first functioning nuclear reactor outside of the United States and an active program of peacetime uses.

By the end of the War, the dispute over uranium appeared to be symbolic of Canada's place between Britain and America. The old ties with Britain had loosened as Canada's natural alliance with the United States developed and British power continued to decline. At the same time, Canada grew increasingly successful in erecting protective limits to American encroachment on its sovereignty. The old battles, over air space and control of Northwest economic development, faded. Long-range aircraft enhanced the military importance of Anchorage and Fairbanks to the U.S. Air Force and commercial carriers, and left all NWSR airfields but Whitehorse to return gradually to a forlorn supporting role. Economic development in the frigid North turned out to be no more popular there than in any other icy spot on earth and did not benefit from the kind of oil finds that gave Alaska a huge boost. Perhaps the biggest economic contribution to the region was the Alaska Highway itself and the 100,000 tourists it brought each summer.

The Canadian experience with the American occupation of the Northwest promoted greater sensitivity north of the border, and it would never again recede. Nothing better epitomized the new Canadian attitude toward the United States than the period of 1968 to 1984, when Pierre Elliott Trudeau served as Prime Minister of Canada. "We are different from you, and we're different because of you," said the Harvard-trained leader. "Living next to you is in some ways like sleeping with an elephant."

Trudeau intended to keep the elephant in its place. After years of wrangling with the Americans, who disputed Canadian claims to the Arctic Islands because of U.S. interest in using them to defend against the Soviet Union, Trudeau simply and finally declared Canadian sovereignty over them. He extended Canada's maritime borders, forcing the United States to come to an agreement on the limits of the fishing rights of each country. This was not Mackenzie King's Canada any longer.

Speaking in 1972, Trudeau laid out his view of Canada's place:

> By diversifying our interests, first from Britain many years ago, and then, subsequently, from the United States as much as we could, Canada has not foregone our friendship with them and the privileged position that I hope we enjoy with these two countries. In other words, our independence has not been gained at the expense of any previous friendship and it will not be exploited, we are sure, by any irritation of other countries just for the sake of irritation.[344]

Richard M. Nixon, President of the United States at the time, called Trudeau "an asshole." Trudeau, like Nixon running for re-election at the time of his speech, said "I've been called worst things by better people" and won.

In 1975, with Nixon departed in disgrace and Trudeau riding high, Canada became one of the countries forming the Group of Seven, the leading industrial nations of the world, taking its place beside the United States, Britain, Japan, France, Germany, and Italy. Its Gross Domestic Product was less than any other member, though its GDP per capita was about the same as all others except the United States. What had made six into seven was clearly geography. The combination of national wealth, size and location had made it a power to be reckoned with, notwithstanding its relatively small population. This was perhaps Trudeau's crowning international achievement and a clear declaration of independence.[345]

Trudeau sought to reduce American domination of the Canadian economy and culture. Foreign investment in certain enterprises was limited as was foreign content, almost entirely American, on television and print media. He tried to develop new trading relationships with other countries to reduce dependence on the American market. In all of these efforts, he ultimately failed. His successor, Brian Mulroney, moved in the opposite direction and tightened trade relationships with the United States, to the benefit of Canada, through the North American Free Trade Agreement. But Trudeau's terms in office left a sense of independence in Canada that did not wholly dissipate.

At the same time as the U.S. and Canadian leaders were trading barbs, Canada never lost sight of its need to cooperate with the United States on continental defense. It joined in the creation of the North American Air Defense Command or NORAD, headquartered in the United States, where the deputy commander would always be a Canadian general. But unlike Britain, Germany, Italy, Turkey, Japan and Korea as late as 2004, Canada, with the Alcan experience in mind, would not again allow a U.S. military base on its territory. Yet the Alcan Highway relationship itself survived through the Shakwak project.

On September 11, 2001, American air space was closed soon after the attacks with many flights in the air on their way from Europe. Canada immediately agreed to allow foreign flights to land and to provide accommodations for the passengers until they could travel on to the United States. Thousands benefitted from this Canadian action. At the same time, Canadians were among those killed at the World Trade Center in New York.

In the wake of the attacks, President George W. Bush addressed a Joint Session of Congress on September 20, 2001. He spoke of Pakistanis, Israelis, people from India, El Salvador, Iran, Mexico, Japan and Britain. The British Prime Minister, in attendance, was told that "America has no truer friend than Great Britain." Canadian Prime Minister Jean Chrétien, who had virtually begged for a White House visit after Bush had been elected, was stunned by the omission of Canada, and so were many Canadians.

This slight did not stand in the way of a new, two-year agreement between the two countries, concluded on December 5, 2002, to develop "bi-national defence arrangements for North American security." Earlier in the year, apparently without consulting Canada, the United States had announced a proposal for the "Northern Command" in which Canadian troops would be placed under an American general. A storm broke out immediately in the Canadian Parliament, forcing Chrétien to state that "the sovereignty of Canada cannot be taken away by a decision made by the administration of the United States."[346] Under the negotiated arrangement, a Planning Group, located at NORAD headquarters under the leadership of the Canadian deputy commander, was given a broad mandate to propose joint action. The agreement stressed that "each Government continues to exercise control of its respective sovereign territory and to command its national forces...." Yet, a few days later, the Globe and Mail, Canada's leading newspaper, reported that, "according to the deal, U.S. troops will be able to come into Canada to operate under the control of a Canadian officer on a case-by-case basis and only by invitation. Canadian troops will also be available to cross the border into the United States."[347] Despite Canada's common interest with the

United States in continental defense, Chrétien with majority popular support refused to support the U.S.-U.K. war on Iraq, launched just a few months later.

The period following the Al Qaeda attack on the United States showed that the relationship between the United States and Canada continued on the course set during World War II. The Americans persisted in a remarkable lack of sensitivity to Canadian sentiments, and Canada continued to struggle with the conflicts between protecting its sovereignty and its dependence on the American protective shield and, since the creation of a free trade area including both countries, on its market.

CHAPTER 12.

ALASKA AWAKES

Like Canada, the territory of Alaska sought to assert itself against the power of the United States. Unlike Canada, Alaska wanted to become a part of the United States instead of being an occupied land, but also wanted self-government. Alcan would help Alaska, but only as part of a larger development: the militarization of the North.

During the construction period, Alaska suffered most of the same fate as the Canadian Northwest. But the Inland region of Alaska was sparsely populated and was the scene of only a small part of the total project, making the total impact far less severe. Perhaps the greatest direct effect was on the natives, much as in Canada. Asked to participate in the fiftieth anniversary celebration of the Alcan Highway, Charles Cross, a native from Tanacross, Alaska said:

> I don't see where, in this '92 you know, where the Native people would celebrate it, because there's nothing for them to celebrate.... We should look at the past and see the damage that's been done to our Native people and their subsistence-style living. Because ... they can't fit into the old way of living, they can't fit into the White people's society, a lot of them, so they're stuck in the middle.[348]

Despite the high priority that Roosevelt assigned to the Alcan Highway, its contribution to the defense of Alaska was far less significant than the sea and air routes. Because the sea lanes were never seriously jeopardized, most men and materiel went to Alaska by ship through the Inland Passage. Aircraft and additional personnel flew the NWSR.

The Alaska Highway was never pushed to its limits and was completed just as the Army began a drastic reduction in its forces in Alaska.

As Washington grew to understand the limits of Japanese military and naval potential, American leaders drew back from their reflexive reaction that Alaska would play a central, strategic role in the War. Never really threatened, despite the diversionary invasion of the Aleutians, Alaska's greatest military contribution was the airway that transported Lend Lease aircraft to the Soviet Union. So, after having provided a backup supply route for the winter of 1942-43, the Alcan Highway began to fade in military value.

The construction of the Alcan Highway and the Japanese occupation of Kiska and Attu raised American awareness of the remote and lightly populated territory that was still "Seward's folly," an unnecessary purchase of a vast, frozen and useless land. These events put Alaska in the news, and thousands of soldiers, assigned there in 1942, greatly increased the number of Americans with first-hand experience of the remote territory.

The military build-up in Alaska, of which the Alcan Highway was only a small part, was enormous. In 1940, about 500 out of the total population of 73,000 was military. Just three years later, the population of 233,000 included 152,000 military personnel. Armed Forces personnel declined to 60,000 two years later and to merely 19,000 after the War.

But, as the most popular history of Alaska would record, "...the war had a profound and lasting impact on the territory. It irrevocably altered the pace and tenor of Alaskan life."[349] The American Government had spent over $1 billion on Alaska during the war, and some of that spending built an infrastructure that would yield benefit to the civilian economy. The contribution was psychological as well as economic, as a display at an Anchorage museum later reported: "The Alaska Highway broke the old territorial shell of isolation and helped transform Alaska into a state in 1959."

Without question, the war brought the realization to the Defense Department that Alaska could have major military value and should be included in future planning. Major facilities that had been developed during the war, including huge airfields near Anchorage and Fairbanks as well as an Army base also near Fairbanks were not abandoned and would later see more forces assigned to them. The long-term military commitment meant that, for the first time, Alaska would have a year-round economic base.

Gradually the issue of Alaska statehood gained congressional interest. At first, objections seemed to outweigh the arguments of Alaska advocates. Some opponents said population was too small, although it was larger than the number of people in other territories when they gained statehood. Others targeted the seasonal economy, although the military presence refuted the concern. Still others said that all states should be contiguous and that Alaska could never rise above commonwealth status. The Alaska Highway was used to rebut that argument, because it provided a land connection with the Lower 48. The major Seattle interests with a stake in the Alaska economy and its resources objected on the grounds that their taxes would increase and their dominance would decrease if a local government existed to pay closer attention to their activities. Finally, the Defense Department, which had stimulated interest in the territory but wanted to maintain a free hand in its use, argued against statehood.

Hawaiian statehood was debated at the same time, but it encountered fewer objections. Its population was larger, and it had a more diversified economy. Hawaii, too, was heavily dependent on the Armed Forces, but the Defense Department made no claims designed to derail its statehood. It certainly was not contiguous, but somehow, nobody raised that issue.

The problem was political. In the U.S. Senate, conservative Republicans and southern Democrats opposed both

Hawaii and Alaska. Each was presumed to be ready to add two senators, more liberal than these groups, which would water down their influence. For some, the inclusion of states where minority groups were either the majority or close to it was not acceptable. The G.O.P., with President Eisenhower in office after 1952, saw Alaska as likely to vote Democratic and consequently found problems with its seeking statehood that did not arise in the case of supposedly Republican Hawaii. The end came only when the less conservative (and sometimes more liberal) northern and eastern senators had grown in number, so that with moderate Republicans, they could control the agenda. Alaska became a state in 1959, even more noncontiguous Hawaii a year later.

The political forecasts turned out to be all wrong. In Washington, Hawaii turned out to be overwhelmingly Democratic, while Alaska lined up consistently with the Republicans. The military invasion of Alaska, begun by the Alcan projects, had finally paid off in changing the state's demographics. In 1940, the Southeast region, including Juneau and populated heavily by government employees and natives accounted for 35 percent of the state's population and was Democratic. By 1960, the second year of statehood, the Anchorage region, home to many newcomers, was 48 percent of the population. Many of the new residents and military retirees brought their Republicanism with them.

During the war, the United States had warned Canada of the Soviet threat and sought to entice Canada with the prospect of an integrated, if American dominated, drive for economic development. While Canada demurred, the United States was free to pursue the same objectives in a territory it controlled. The rapid reduction in the American military presence in Alaska implied that the concern about Soviet intentions was less acute than Washington had told Ottawa. Only after the opening of the Korean conflict in 1950 did the United States begin a military buildup in Alaska that would result in a significant ongoing commitment there. Ultimately, a full Infantry regiment was permanently stationed in Alaska as well as two large Air Force bases. In the end, Alaska's location became a strategic factor, long after Alcan was all but forgotten.

The kind of economic development for which the United States sought a privileged position in Canada never developed in Alaska any more than it had in Canada. The Prudhoe Bay oil discoveries transformed the Alaskan economy, but as the oil supplies are depleted, the state's future appears to depend on opening more oilfields. Without more oil, the economy could falter, and a decline in the state's population would be possible.

Somewhat curiously, the Alcan route offered part of the potential solution to the depletion of oil reserves. Large quantities of natural gas were found on the Alaska North Slope. Natural gas could resuscitate the Alaskan economy as oil was depleted. In 1977, under President Jimmy Carter and Prime Minister Trudeau, the United States and Canada signed a treaty to authorize the construction of a natural gas pipeline from Prudhoe Bay to Fairbanks and then to follow the Alaska Highway to connect with a pipeline into the Lower 48. This Alaska Natural Gas Transmission System would first carry Alaska natural gas, but Canada could connect its Mackenzie Delta gas to it as well.

The first portion of the project, bringing southern Canadian natural gas into the United States was built and operates. But nothing more happened. The Alaska natural gas producers found that the project was not feasible without a subsidy from the U.S. Government or American natural gas customers. Coming under strong pressure from other American producers, Congress refused to authorize any subsidy for the ANGTS. The Canadians decided that the route was unsatisfactory, as Canadian interests would have to pay the full costs of bringing gas down from Mackenzie. Canada then proposed that the line should take a different route across the top of Alaska and Canada to pick up gas from both areas, before turning south.

In November 2002, Alaskans voted to authorize the construction of a natural gas pipeline entirely within the state to be connected to a liquified natural gas terminal to allow shipping the fuel out of the state by tanker. One of the contractors on the LNG terminal would be the omnipresent Bechtel. Although not considered likely to be built, the proposed pipeline was aimed at scolding Canada for wanting to use a line across its own territory for its own natural gas. Scott Hepworth, a longshoreman who led the campaign for the Alaska-only project, told his victorious supporters: "I don't want to bring pain to Canada but my allegiance has to belong to Alaska...."[350] In an ultimate irony, the highway to Alaska was finally spurned, perhaps with some justification, by Alaska.

In the end, the Alaska Highway's role in Alaska left it just another road and not the most important one in a state that has so few roads that they go by name not number. Little freight is transported by road between Alaska and the Lower 48. The principal means of freight transport remains West Coast shipping, and there are several heavily used ports. Some freight enters by air. As for passengers, in the summer of 2001, of the 1,675,800 people arriving in Alaska, only 74,584 passed through the Alcan Highway entry point, just 4.5 percent.

The route of the Alaska Highway had once been highly contested, as states and commercial interests vied for what they thought would be a bonanza. But there would be no big payoff.

CHAPTER 13.

SONS OF THE MIDDLE BORDER

Fifty years of movies have depicted World War II as a period of unalloyed patriotism, with Americans marching shoulder to shoulder in the spirit of mutual sacrifice. It may have looked that way on the white side of the color line. But for African-Americans, the war ushered in one of the most bitter periods of the modern era, thanks to the policy of military segregation that barred most black soldiers from combat and poisoned relations between black Americans and the federal government.[351]

Written by a commentator in *The New York Times* sixty years after the Alcan, these words reflected the depth of feeling of black soldiers. The treatment of these soldiers, wasteful of a willing and able military resource with great potential to shorten the war, was a textbook case of institutional and ingrained racism.

A band of American territory just 280 miles wide by 35 miles across the middle of the Civil War border states of Missouri and Kansas, both slave states, was the home of five men, three of whom defended segregation in the Army and two who ended it. Four of these "Sons of the Middle Border"[352] – Bradley, Eisenhower, Hoge and Maxwell Taylor — were generals, and one — Truman — was President of the United States. Bradley and Hoge would fight black aspirations to the last; Eisenhower would be a supporting actor in the drama who was ultimately unwilling to challenge the old ways; Truman would lead the way to change and Taylor and his postwar colleagues would make change happen.

The foundation for the final big battle of the war against Army segregation was built in part by the gains made by black soldiers as a result of their segregated participation in the war. Two-thirds of the black soldiers in World War II came from the segregated South, where they had been deprived of education, health care, opportunity and justice. The Army provided a degree of progress in all of these areas, although hardly to the level enjoyed by whites. On the Alcan projects, black soldiers received the same rations and the same housing as white troops and had access to the same medical care. They were not subject to discrimination in the distribution of the Army's basic services, and many received a better level of nourishment and care than they had experienced at home. Despite segregation and their assignment to only a supporting role, their experience would contribute to a "revolution of rising expectations."

The victims of the harshest form of segregation in the South came into contact for the first time with blacks from the North, people who were used to being able to assert their rights, with some success. When black soldiers spoke out against abuses at the hands of the Army and suffered much less drastic consequences than in Dixie, soldiers from the South began to learn about the virtues of protest. As Northern troops began to receive copies of black newspapers from Chicago or Pittsburgh, soldiers from the South learned of the struggle of blacks in civilian society against continued racism.

Contacts among black soldiers led many from the South to plan for a postwar life in the North. In an Army survey, more than half of the black enlisted men said they would not go home again, with 41 percent planning to settle in the North and another 11 percent wanting to go West. [353]

Not only had Northern blacks experienced less segregation and demonstrated more reluctance to accept the Army's brand of racism, but they were generally better educated than the Southerners. Among black soldiers from the North, about 20 percent of privates and 35 per cent of noncommissioned officers had graduated high school, while only

10 percent of the privates and just over 20 percent of the non-coms from the South had a similar educational background.[354] Given the much higher presence of black southerners, the largest single group of black enlisted men were southerners with only a grade school education and probably much of that education was inferior. Many Northern blacks took on the task of teaching these soldiers to read and write. Some of the white officers assumed the same responsibility and put them on the path to literacy.[355] A black soldier assisting a white dentist was surprised one day when the officer even offered to pay his way to dental school.[356]

Despite these positive signs, morale among black soldiers was much lower than among whites. They encountered discrimination regularly from white officers, many of them Southerners. They had little opportunity for advancement, and almost never encountered black officers, other than their chaplains. They knew that, with few exceptions, black soldiers were being denied the right to serve in combat, but were relegated to support units. Somewhat oddly, after suffering so much discrimination themselves and even seeing German and Italian POWs treated better than they were, many black soldiers desperately wanted to see combat action.

The black units engaged in the Alcan projects fared better than most black troops, as all were sent on to greater responsibility in the war effort. The 93rd Regiment was assigned to assisting in dislodging the Japanese from the Aleutians and preventing further incursions, the 97th was assigned to the Pacific war zone, the 95th and 388th were sent to European combat zones. While none was converted into a combat unit, they benefitted from their Alcan experience in getting better assignments, closer to the action.

Sometimes the wall of segregation crumbled. Officer Candidate Schools, with the exception of those for pilots, were not segregated. In a curious way, the Army recognized that "separate but equal" would not work in training officers moving up from the enlisted ranks. It found that there was no basis for providing different training based on race, because it did not want to run the risk that black officers would be asked to meet a lower standard. And separate training schools were less efficient. But that consideration did not reach the Air Corps, where the separation maintained for pilots seemed to have reflected the Air Corps' desire to prevent blacks from actually flying aircraft in combat.

The policy of having only one OCS system was a limited success as few blacks were assigned to these schools, because local commanders blocked applications from black soldiers. Some supporters of black rights called for an OCS quota system, which the Army firmly opposed. Segregationists opposed integrated OCS facilities located in areas where the races in the civilian population were kept separate. And, because black officers were not allowed to command white troops, demand for them was limited. Probably the most well-known product of the OCS system that admitted blacks was Jackie Robinson, although his Army service was cut short when he protested being forced to ride in the back of a bus on an Army post.

Of greater significance, the other loophole in the Army's policy of segregation came late in the war in the European Theater of Operations, a combat area. "In combat, black and white soldiers got along fine," said one of the black soldiers from the 95th, who served in Europe. In one incident, when a group of white soldiers arrived in a pub looking for blacks who had caused them some offense, the white soldiers who had worked side-by-side with the blacks jumped to their defense. "We had a shared experience," the black soldier said, "and had saved each others' lives."[357] However, on the troop ship going back home such camaraderie dissipated.

What happened to this soldier was happening on a much larger scale by 1945, the final year of the war. As the Army advanced across Europe toward Germany in late 1944, it began to run short of combat soldiers. At the same time, support units, some of them black, had surplus troops. The imbalance resulted in large part from the policy of segregation, because the Army's policy that the percentage of blacks in the service should equal their share of the civilian population of the same age was coupled with assigning blacks mainly to service units, which created an oversupply of troops in those units.

White service troops had begun to be reassigned to combat units, making the situation of the black units even more deplorable. Gen. Dwight D. Eisenhower was by then commander of all U.S. forces in Europe and in late 1944 one of his generals recommended that black service troops be allowed to apply for training and assignment as individuals in white units. Eisenhower agreed and, on December 26, 1944, the call went out for volunteers. As soon as it was circulated, others around Eisenhower warned him that he must report his action to Washington, which would not want to see its segregationist policy undermined.

Eisenhower declined to inform Washington but found a way around the problem. He withdrew the special call for black volunteers and replaced it with a general appeal including the statement that "in the event that the number of suitable negro volunteers exceeds the replacement needs of negro combat units, these men will be suitably incorporated in other organizations so that their service and their fighting spirit may be efficiently utilized."[358]

The troops were to be retrained for infantry service with existing black units, but there were no black Infantry units in Europe, and Eisenhower knew that. Despite the language of his statement, the blacks would be assigned, not as individuals, but formed into platoons that would be integrated into companies of white troops. A platoon might be less than 30 soldiers, only a tiny portion of a 1,000 person regiment, so Eisenhower was effectively breaking the rule that blacks should not be assigned in units smaller than regiments. The Supreme Commander had not suddenly decided to attack the traditional Army policy of segregation. That policy simply was inefficient, and now faced with the tough final resistance of the Germans and high casualties sustained between D-Day and the Battle of the Bulge, Eisenhower could not afford to waste any resources. Eisenhower was making a landmark decision on the basis of efficiency, but seemed not to have fully realized its implications.

The flood of black volunteers was so great that the Army had to turn back more than it accepted. The 2,500 troops selected for the Infantry yielded 53 platoons, well more than two regiments in the aggregate, and they were assigned to combat. In some cases, the platoons were organized into black companies and the lack of preparation for this use was evident by the lower performance than in the integrated companies. When the war in Europe ended in May 1945, so did the integrated units. But for five months, one theater of operations had been integrated.

Immediately after V-E Day, the Army conducted a survey of white officers and sergeants on the performance of the black rifle platoons.[359] Only about a third of each group originally had been favorable to serving in an integrated company. Asked if their opinions had changed, 77 per cent of both officers and sergeants said that they had become more favorable to black soldiers on the basis of their experience. Not one single respondent said he was less favorable.

More than 80 percent of the officers and noncommissioned officers found that black soldiers had done "very well," the highest rating, with virtually all others giving them the next highest rating. Asked to compare white and black infantry soldiers, only about 5 percent of each group said they were not as good as white troops, while 17 per cent of the officers and 9 percent of the NCOs said they were better than white troops. As for the ability of black and white soldiers to get along together, 73 percent of the officers and 60 percent of the NCOs said they got along "fairly well." The report notes that "actual friction between white and colored soldiers is said to have been confined to isolated cases involving white soldiers from 'outside' units who did not know the combat record of the colored troops. Evidence indicates that white and colored soldiers have gotten along best together in those units in which they have shared the heaviest combat."

Finally, the interviewees were asked the best way of assigning black soldiers. Most popular was the way it had been done, a black platoon in a white company, with 89 per cent of NCOs supporting that format. Only 7 percent of the officers and 1 percent of the NCOs favored complete integration on an individual basis. The most frequently cited reason for preferring platoons was that they encouraged friendly competition. The second most mentioned reason was to prevent friction "because of the old feeling of boys from the South." Because of the somewhat startling results, the survey staff stressed that the blacks had been volunteers, implying, without support, that volunteers would do better in combat than draftees.

The question immediately arose about publishing these results, which ran so sharply against the grain of Army policy. Somervell, a native of Arkansas, opposed their release on the grounds that, according to his inaccurate statement, only 1,000 blacks had been involved, which was not enough to count as a valid test. He worried that the NAACP might pick up the results and use them to demand similar treatment of blacks in the Pacific theater of operations. Above all, he was concerned that members of Congress and the press who opposed integration and on whom the Army depended might prevent universal military training, a continuation of the draft, after the war.

Gen. Omar N. Bradley, a son of the middle border and leader of American field forces in Europe, was even more negative. The units had only participated in second-rate ground operations, he thought, and the troops were volunteers, more intelligent than the average black. He said that the whites and blacks had not actually gotten along well when not on the front line. In light of the survey results, his influence in denying its conclusions was really a matter of rank above reason. If the experiment were tried again, he would revert to black companies in white regiments. This proposal was an obvious rearguard action. Gen. Marshall, unwilling at any time to argue with his subordinates over race issues, accepted the comments of both Somervell and Bradley and suppressed the survey.[360]

When the war ended, black soldiers and the U.S. Army went their separate ways, with almost all of the troops going back to civilian life. Army surveys revealed that 37 percent of black soldiers were interested in government jobs after the war compared with only 17 percent among whites. While the overall number of soldiers expecting to work for government at some level was about the same as had left such work for war, the racial mixture of those employed by government was likely to include far more blacks. The surveys found that many soldiers could not distinguish clearly between government and civilian work, but those who wanted to work for the government sought "the security which seems inherent in large scale operations." Perhaps the black soldiers understood well enough that they would get better job protection at the federal level, because their interest in federal employment far outstripped the whites'.[361]

Anecdotal evidence suggests that, while many blacks returned to the kind of employment they had led before the war, a significant share took advantage of the training they had received to seek jobs with the U.S. Post Office. Veteran's preference helped them secure good paying and secure employment there.

But some of these veterans continued to face systematic discrimination. The experience of Jesse Balthazar, a veteran of the 97th Engineers who had qualified for OCS but had been denied assignment, illustrated the problems the black veterans faced. Hired by the Post Office, he arrived at the Houston Post Office to find that the black letter carriers' "swing room" was packed tight, while the larger room for whites gave them more than enough space. Eventually, the black carriers got the bigger room, but they could not get promoted. Balthazar had passed the supervisor's exam with a good score, but never got the job. Finally, in 1966, the year after the passage of the landmark Voting Rights Act, the black labor union told him that he had passed with the highest score, but did not get promoted because his supervisors, always whites, would not recommend him. A Roman Catholic, he went to his priest who in turn talked with the Houston Postmaster, also a Catholic. Balthazar was soon called and told he had the appointment as supervisor, a position he held until his retirement in 1972. Such were the rewards for an obviously capable black soldier: no OCS and promotion in his federal job only 21 years after the war.[362]

Blacks going back to the South, often encountered a level of racism even greater than when they had gone to war and much more serious than the kind of employment discrimination encountered by Balthazar. Racist Southerners took steps to make sure that, whatever their wartime experience, blacks had gained no additional rights and were entitled to no better treatment than when they had left. Some Southern whites were alarmed by demands by returning black veterans for greater democracy and the right to register to vote. The best way to reject those demands and discourage such claims was through acts of repression including lynching. While less extreme, the reaction in some areas of the North was also negative. The Ku Klux Klan rose to the surface, and race riots seemed imminent.

On February 12, 1946, Sergeant Isaac Woodard, a black soldier from the Bronx, New York, had just been discharged from the Army and was traveling on a bus through Batesburg, South Carolina, on his way back home. He was taken from the bus by Lynwood Lanier Shull, the local police chief, on grounds that he was disturbing the peace. By the next morning, Woodard had been severely beaten by the chief with one of his eyes gouged out and the other so damaged that he was blinded in both eyes. Shull did not deny his actions. He had sent a strong message to returning black veterans.

For the first time, such an action in a Southern state would not be ignored in Washington. The difference was that Harry Truman was now President. Although one single event may not have decided him to move against segregation in the armed forces, the Woodard case might have been the trigger.

Truman, though opposed to social equality for blacks and not reluctant to use a racist vocabulary, had a simple view of what was coming to be known as civil rights as early as 1940 when he ran for reelection to the Senate. That year, he told a white audience: "I believe in the brotherhood of man; not merely the brotherhood of white men, but the brotherhood of all men before the law.... The majority of our Negro people find but cold comfort in shanties and tenements. Surely, as freemen, they are entitled to something better than this."[363] He told a black audience that he favored equality before the law for the black man, "because he is a human being and a natural born American."[364]

Engaged in a close primary election, which he barely won, Truman might be pandering to the black vote. But he had spoken to his white audience in the heart of the Middle Border, not in St. Louis or Kansas City. And he had intervened to thwart discrimination against black soldiers at nearby Fort Leavenworth. These actions went far beyond the needs of catering to the black vote, which he received. He had begun to show signs that defeating discrimination was a matter of principle as well of politics for him. During 1941, the first year of his new term, he introduced a bill calling for General Benjamin Davis to be assigned to a combat command. The bill went nowhere.

The Woodard case and the gunning down of two black veterans and their wives in Georgia had a special significance for Truman. His service as captain of Battery D in France in World War I had been a turning point in his life. Elected by his soldiers to be their captain, he found he was a natural leader, and he came to love the Army and his unit and to treasure his experience. He did not see Woodard and the others primarily as blacks; they were veterans. In Truman's view, if you had put your life on the line for your country, you deserved special respect, not racist brutality.

Truman only learned of the Woodard case in September 1946 and within a week the U.S. Justice Department began a civil rights action against Shull. While the use of the Constitution to fight race-based criminal offenses would

become more common 20 years later, this action was virtually unprecedented. Not surprisingly, a South Carolina jury,
all of its members white, found Shull, who admitted his
actions, not guilty and took only 30 minutes to reach its verdict.

The President would not take this verdict for a final
answer. On December 5, 1946, he named the President's
Committee on Civil Rights to determine the extent of the
civil rights problems and to make recommendations for
presidential and congressional action to deal with them.
Two parts of his announcement were especially striking:
something must be done to protect black veterans and the
15-member Committee included two black members.

The American people were not clamoring for such a
committee. A national poll found that 66 percent of American whites thought blacks were being treated fairly, while
only 25 percent thought they were not. The mirror image
showed that 66 percent of blacks thought they were not
being treated fairly. Although the sincerity of Truman's con-
viction has not been seriously disputed, he also had political
considerations in mind. In 1944, many blacks saw the
replacement of Vice President Henry Wallace, a strong civil
rights advocate, by Truman as a sellout, based on their
belief that Truman was tainted by his Missouri background.
With an eye to the next presidential election, Truman
wanted to let the black community know of his personal
convictions on civil rights.

In 1945 the Army had begun to review its policies
toward blacks. At the urging of Truman Gibson, Judge
Hastie's successor in the War Department, Robert Patterson,
now the Secretary of War, created a Board headed by General Alvan C. Gillem Jr. to review these policies. In April
1946, the Gillem Board reported that the Army had not used
black troops efficiently in World War II. The report did not
oppose segregation, but called for the kind of unit integration that had been used by Eisenhower and for equal opportunity for black officers. The Army adopted the
recommendations; it did not implement them. Maintaining

purely black units, while seeking to have 10 percent of the
Army composed of blacks, resulted in the traditional inefficiency of World War II. Nobody was more honest that integration was going nowhere than Kenneth Royall, the North
Carolina native who had succeeded Patterson, who said that
the Army's policy was "equality of opportunity on the basis
of segregation."[365]

On October 29, 1947, the Committee sent to the President its recommendations calling for civil rights protection
to be placed in the Department of Justice, an anti-lynching
law, voting rights and Fair Employment Practices Commission — all major civil rights initiatives. The Committee also
finally revealed the results of the survey of white officers
and sergeants after the 1945 use of black infantry platoons
in Europe. The Committee recommended congressional
actions to end segregation in the Armed Forces, especially
now that a single Department of Defense had been created.
Unlike the military leadership, it found that the Armed
Forces should be used to promote social change.

At the same time, the political backdrop was changing.
Traditionally all of the concern about the reaction of white
Americans to the Army's policy on using black soldiers had
focused on the South. Powerful members of Congress, who
could determine military funding, were among the most
staunch segregationists and had to be placated. But in 1947,
the North began to make strong demands for a change in
policy.

National Guard units, even those in Northern states,
were segregated, but demands now came from the North for
change. General Eisenhower, having risen to become the
Army Chief of Staff, continued the ban on integration, but
said that black companies could be part of white battalions,
less integration than he himself had permitted in 1945. In
early 1948, the governor of New Jersey announced that the
Army had vetoed integration of the state's National Guard,
despite a provision of the state constitution banning discrimination in the state militia, the National Guard.[366] Other

states, including New York, the home of Truman's likely Republican opponent in 1948, joined in.

Coupled with these internal pressures were foreign policy concerns. Truman had quickly come to understand that the cold war would result in a battle for support among nations where a majority of the population was not white and where American actions would be measured against Soviet propaganda. The United States would need the support of the black community both to supply the Armed Forces with personnel and to show a more progressive American policy.

On February 2, 1948, Truman sent a strong civil rights message to Congress embodying many of the Committee's recommendations. This message did not include proposals for ending segregation in the Armed Forces on the grounds that Truman, as Commander in Chief, could deal with the issue without congressional action. More important, he did not want Congress dealing with segregation when he was trying to get it to pass laws extending the draft and instituting Universal Military Training, issues on which he thought he needed the support of key Southern senators.

Truman continued to hope that the new Department of Defense under James V. Forrestal, a man sympathetic to civil rights who he had named as its first Secretary, might take action without anything more than the Committee report. But Forrestal was more concerned about integration of the Armed Services than racial integration, so he did not want to create complications by raising the segregation issue. He also thought progress should come more gradually than Truman believed the times demanded.

A. Philip Randolph, who had been charged by his own community with having been duped by Roosevelt when he called off his planned 1941 March on Washington, was militant in arguing against the Forrestal position. Testifying on the draft bill, he said that he would advocate that blacks refuse to be conscripted, an exercise in civil disobedience. Even when a senator charged that his position might be treason, he refused to back down, and one survey among

New York blacks backed him up.[367] His position served at least one useful purpose as the draft law was passed without being harassed by a threatened Southern filibuster, but also without ending segregation. The Southerners liked to quote Eisenhower, who had once told a congressional committee: "I do believe that if we attempt merely by passing a lot of laws to force someone to like someone else, we are just going to get into trouble."[368]

Truman was now in trouble. The South knew that he wanted to end segregation in the Army. Once the draft law was passed, the Democratic National Convention in mid-July rejected a vague civil rights platform, favored by Truman, in favor of one championed by Minneapolis Mayor Hubert H. Humphrey calling, among other reforms, for the end of segregation in the Armed Forces. After the vote, the South bolted the convention with entire delegations walking off the floor. Truman was advised to back the platform plank adopted by the convention or risk losing black support, desperately needed. Both Progressive Henry Wallace and Republican Governor Thomas E. Dewey of New York were actively seeking black votes.

On July 26, 1948, Truman issued two Executive Orders. The first required the immediate end of segregation and discrimination in federal employment and set up agencies to enforce this decision. The second relatively brief document, Executive Order 9981, began with a simple command:

> It is hereby declared to be the policy of the President that there shall be equality of treatment and opportunity for all persons in the armed services without regard to race, color, religion, or national origin. This policy shall be put into effect as rapidly as possible having due regard to the time required to effectuate any necessary changes without impairing efficiency or morale.[369]

The order had been reviewed and accepted by Forrestal and Royall as well as Walter White, head of the NAACP, and Randolph. This was not good news, because it meant that it was vague enough to allow conflicting interpretations and lacked a specific date for implementation. In an unusual way, the situation was soon clarified. The day after the Executive Order was issued, General Bradley, the new Army Chief of Staff, told a group of officers that the Army would not desegregate. While he appeared to be ready to resist the President's order, he had not, in fact, heard of it. Still, he did not immediately back down and was hailed by Southern senators for supporting segregation. In reaction, the black press promptly attacked Order 9981 for being too vague. Three days after he had issued the order and undoubtedly forced by the Bradley controversy to state his position, Truman told the press unequivocally that he meant to end segregation in the Armed Forces.[370] In a preview of his later confrontation with General MacArthur, Truman left no doubt that he was the top military commander. Bradley apologized, but the Army under his command never complied with the order.

Army Secretary Royall believed that segregation was not the same as discrimination and fought on. He said that, unless a state law or constitution banned it, the national segregation policy must prevail over state policy requiring integration of its National Guard units. Ultimately, the same argument would cause integration of the National Guard, over Southern objections, when national policy swung behind integration.

The President had appointed a committee to oversee and promote the end of military segregation. The Committee successfully made the case that segregation promoted inefficiency, but could find that only the Air Force had a good program to end it. The Navy was making progress, but the Marines and the Army made almost none. Even Gordon Gray, the new Army Secretary who replaced Royall in 1949, continued to be dominated by generals who wanted to retain segregation. The Committee's work ended in July 1950 without Order 9981 yet being implemented.

In addition to this Committee, Truman had taken one other action that symbolized his commitment to integration. In 1949, he appointed William Hastie, formerly a federal judge in the Virgin Islands, Truman's appointee as Governor there and Stimson's frustrated advisor of Negro affairs, to the Third U.S. Circuit Court of Appeals, the first time a black would serve on the federal judiciary in the continental United States.

By 1950, the Army changed course, but not because of the President's order. Gen. J. Lawton Collins, a Texas native and the son of a general, had been named Army Chief of Staff. He had direct experience with the integrated platoons in 1945 and had made up his mind that integration was more efficient than segregation, right "down the line," although he favored no more than two blacks per squad. In late June 1950, war broke out in Korea.

General Douglas MacArthur, a native of Arkansas, took charge of the allied forces fighting in Korea. Early in the war, Thurgood Marshall, the NAACP Counsel, managed to meet with the renowned general only after Truman's direct intervention and came away with the view that MacArthur was a racist. Meanwhile, the black component of the Army reached ever higher levels, as enlistments increased. They were needed on the lines, but the generals continued to argue that they were of little value in combat.

Maj. Gen. Maxwell D. Taylor, a senior Army staff officer and yet another son of the Middle Border, called for a study of the initial performance of black troops in Korea, and the chief of military personnel went along with his recommendation. The results validated the 1945 survey, showing that integrated units did better than segregated units and that there was little opposition among the soldiers to integration. This time, there could be no valid claim that the numbers involved were too small. Thanks to Taylor's initiative, the Army's own study provided the Secretary of the Army and the Chief of Staff with the basis to order integration of the grounds of military necessity. In mid-1951, General Matthew Ridgway, a Virginian who had replaced MacArthur as the head of U.N. troops in Korea, abolished segregation in the Army units under his command. On

October 30, 1954, the last segregated unit in any of the regular armed forces was disbanded.

The debate between reason and racism had at last been resolved. The Army officer corps, dominated by Southerners who, for the most part, had claimed that separation of the races was more efficient, opposed moving toward integration, because they argued that the Army should not be an instrument of social change. Gradually, experience showed that the officer corps supported segregation as a matter of social policy, and that its supposed inefficiency could not be supported by the facts. As for social policy, the National Guard issue had revealed that, just as the South had resisted any notion of integrated military units in its territory, the North had come to resist anything less than integration in its territory. White soldiers seemed to be less concerned about integration than were the white generals.

The Army has come to represent one of the best examples of race blindness in American society. Like Southerners after the Civil War who saw the Army as a path from poverty to success, blacks after Korea have used it to gain education, economic strength and public esteem. Yet problems remain, as black officers in the senior officer grades are promoted less often than white. A major reason is that many black officers emerge from ROTC units at historically black campuses, where white officers frequently do not serve.[371] As on the Alcan projects, leadership is critical to success, especially leadership by the white officers who will dominate the promotion selection process.

At the fiftieth anniversary ceremony of the black soldiers who had worked on the Alcan projects, Bishop Edward Carroll, one of the few black officers who had been there, said: "I volunteered to be a chaplain ... for the purpose of helping men keep true perspective concerning the defense of freedom. I wanted to help black soldiers overcome the stigma of being used only as labor battalions fit only for pick and shovel work...." The stigma had been lifted only by war itself.

Part VI. Alcan and Al Qaeda

Chapter 14.

Unlearned Lessons

The ultimate crisis for the United States or any country is a surprise attack on its territory. However terrible the death and destruction, even greater is the damage to the national spirit caused by fear itself — fear of further attacks, fear of the unknown, fear of losing.

Alcan was an impressive, almost reflexive, part of America's response to Pearl Harbor and one of many Rooseveltian gestures to suppress fear and nurture confidence among the American people. The Alcan experience, although only one of a number of reactions, embodied the central elements inherent in such an attack and the response to it: the failure of intelligence, the compulsion to overreact, and the sacrifice of democratic values on the alter of efficiency.

Franklin D. Roosevelt called fear "nameless", because so often, and inevitably in an attack on the homeland, people cannot grasp fully what has happened, and their lack of understanding heightens their apprehension. Millions of words have been spilled about the element of surprise at Pearl Harbor. But it remains worth remembering that intelligence failed on both sides of the Pacific because of the failure of each country to understand, through an informed appreciation of the other's culture, the driving forces behind their national aspirations.

In 1935, Japan's democratic government, which had sent its best young men to be educated in the United States, was overthrown by a military coup, unchallenged by the Emperor. The new Tokyo government was imbued with the desire to expand the Empire so it could control the resource base on which the home islands depended. The new regime shunted aside those who understood how to achieve national objectives through diplomacy and replaced such skills with a policy of aggression based on brute force. Yet the United States continued to believe that Japan would listen to reason, and that diplomacy could solve the deepening crisis between the two countries. It preferred to believe that because there were Japanese diplomats, there must be Japanese diplomacy. This failure to fully appreciate the changes taking place across the Pacific meant that Japan could get away with a surprise bombing of the U.S. Pacific fleet while Japanese envoys sat in the office of the Secretary of State.

The Japanese, while aware of the potential of American production, also misunderstood their adversary. They counted on fear to breed despair, so that the United States would acquiesce in Japanese expansion rather than respond with force to dislodge a foe occupying vast Pacific territories. They saw a country that had already experienced the depths of such despair in the Great Depression, which had not yet completely ended. But the United States, rallied by an eloquent and seemingly ever-confident president, overcame despondency to unleash its production and to deploy its forces at an undreamed-of pace and to launch within six months the stinging counterattack at Midway.

The self-confidence asked of the American people was blind, because, even after Pearl Harbor, the U.S. Government did not understand Japanese intentions and capabilities and consequently was forced to plan for the worst case. Japanese expansionism was no longer in doubt; it remained for the Americans to figure out how far the Empire was capable of taking it. Out of the depths of its ignorance, Washington had to assume that Alaska would be attacked. Resources, economic and human, were allocated unstintingly, including the deployment of 10,000 men to the Canadian Northwest and Alaska in less than two months.

Intelligence is not perfect, and it cannot be perfect, because the cost to civil liberties of trying to make it so would be too high. Intelligence remains as much an art as a science. Still, perhaps it needs to borrow more from the scientific method: the intelligence community would not seek to prove that a hypothesis was true, but would attempt to disprove a given hypothesis. Instead of believing that an attack on Pearl Harbor was impossible, intelligence agencies would have assumed that Hawaii could be attacked by the Japanese and then sought evidence to disprove definitively this hypothesis. If they could not do so satisfactorily, they would be left with the working assumption that an attack could be launched on Pearl Harbor. Similarly, once the Japanese had attacked American territory, they could assume another attack was possible, as they did, but then seek to disprove that hypothesis, as they did not, even in the face of mounting evidence that such an attack was beyond Japanese capabilities.

Attacks like Pearl Harbor or 9/11 are called "unthinkable," and in their wake government says that it must "think the unthinkable," and consider that such attacks are possible, even likely. The use of the scientific method might have helped the United States to understand better the scope of Japanese ambitions and the Empire's abilities to realize those ambitions. Yet, if politics or bureaucratic infighting, as in the case of the Midway Hypo code breakers, intervene to distort the exercise or dictate the results, the effort would be rendered worthless.

But because intelligence, even if it can be improved, remains imperfect, surprise attacks are as inevitable and impossible to prevent as political assassinations. We must assume that the attack on Pearl Harbor and the fear in early 1942 that Alaska might also be a target were unavoidable. What was the nature of the response?

"Certainly, no one has ever accused democracies of being particularly efficient in their deliberations," says a primer on democracy distributed by the U.S. State Department. Democracy is intended to be inefficient so as to prevent the tyranny of the majority, the democratic abuse of power. Yet efficiency is just what seems to be needed in responding to a surprise attack. Suddenly, government must function on a larger scale and at greater speed than is customary in the routine functioning of democracy.

Efficiency, embodying the principles of magnification — working bigger — and acceleration — working faster, nudges aside democratic norms. Both an effective response and public morale seem to require a sudden, if temporary, transformation of the political ethic.

Article II, Section 2 of the U.S. Constitution provides that the president is the "Commander in Chief" of the armed forces. When this article was written, George Washington was expected to be the first President, and the framers clearly thought that the chief of the executive branch should serve as a military leader with extraordinary powers. In times of crisis since Washington, the president has assumed the role of supreme war leader virtually automatically and without challenge. Having a figure to rally around also comforts the people. In this role the president acts as head of state, a position all Americans can support, rather than as head of government, which would expose him or her to political debate. Of course, a skillful president like Roosevelt can mix the two roles, enabling him to take politically advantageous actions with little or no opposition.

In a democracy, this unusual grant of power is temporary, and the leader may later pay a price for it. While Roosevelt did not live to see the end of the war, Churchill was ousted by British voters even before it was completely ended. Truman acted forcefully in responding to the North Korean invasion of South Korea in 1950, but stood no chance of winning the next presidential election.

The president's assertion of his powers as Commander in Chief solves the problem of the separation of powers, raised by the existence of Congress and inherent in the American system of government, but absent in countries with parliamentary systems, such as Britain and Canada, where the government usually controls the legislative majority. Lincoln actively carried out his role as Commander in Chief, and his difficult experience with the Joint

Committee on the Conduct of the War demonstrated that strategy and tactics cannot be determined by an unwieldy legislative body. Congress cannot control the war effort and is likely to become no more than a rubber stamp. The Truman Committee was such an aberration from the general rule against congressional involvement that its unusual success serves to explain how an obscure, machine politician from Missouri could become president. It also reflected Roosevelt's great political skills, because he knew that Truman understood his limits and could provide a useful, relief valve for war critics. The Truman Committee helped save money, but the Army's ability to finance Canol in the summer on 1944, well after its futility had been fully demonstrated, showed the limits of its powers. No such committee has ever again existed.

In fighting the war, Roosevelt was assisted only by a small and exclusive group of people. The need to prevent endless debate about strategy makes this approach efficient, but it can serve to exclude dissenters or those with perspectives different from the core group. After Pearl Harbor, the United States adopted informally the practice of the British and Canadians and created what was effectively a War Cabinet, a handful of people to make virtually all of the major decisions about the conduct of the war. At the core of this group were the Secretaries of State, War and the Navy, with others joining as needed or when Roosevelt wanted to use an old and loyal political friend. Congress was not represented in this group.

Even in the president's select War Cabinet, conflicts arose. The defense establishment and the diplomatic establishment would inevitably clash. While the official line of communications with Canada ran through the State Department, the Canadian Department of External Affairs and the embassies, the Army frequently ignored this connection in favor of direct action, often without even informing the Canadians. The urgent requirements of a war effort, at least in the eyes of the War Department, meant that "diplomatic niceties" had to be ignored. The military's immediate needs

blinded it to diplomacy's longer view of international relationships. The Army did not see the advantages of present-
ing issues in terms that might facilitate acceptance by
another country and, even more importantly, insure its support later. American hopes for postwar involvement in Canada were undermined by the manner in which the Army
"occupied" the Canadian Northwest. To take just one example: the use of commercial airlines to transport troops gave
rise to suspicions about the long-term intentions of the airline companies, which lead ultimately to the denial of the
postwar air rights in Canada sought by the U.S. Government. The Army's preemptive, short-term actions resulted
in short-term successes, achieved without regard to the
resentment they caused nor its long-term consequences.

Though not on the relatively exalted level of the mili-
tary-diplomatic conflicts, turf battles, ever-present in government, became more acute as the stakes increased in time
of maximum peril. The War Department took on all comers.
It asserted its right to build the Alcan projects over the
objections of the Navy Department. It deceived and fought
relentlessly with the Interior Department and other war
resources agencies. The Army Engineers tangled with the
PRA. While the Army justified its tactics on the grounds
that it knew best what was needed to win the war and to
support its troops, it occasionally lost its compass and
opposed other agencies beyond the bounds of reason and
occasionally to its own detriment, as when Ickes delayed
Somervell's acquisition of the oil refinery the general
wanted for Canol. These bureaucratic tussles seldom
reached the public's purview, but they incurred substantial
costs.

The President and his War Cabinet reacted to Pearl Harbor by mobilizing a war effort adequate to prevent further
attacks and, eventually, to recover what was lost. Force had
to be met with force, and the aggressor warned and ultimately punished. To achieve these objectives with certainly,
the response had to exceed the minimum actually needed to
get the job done. An effective response to the Japanese

attacks across the Pacific required an immediate demonstration of the country's economic and military strength and of its ability to mobilize rapidly; Alcan was a key element of that mobilization message. No thought could be given, at least initially, to the real need for it.

Not only must a message, backed by a substantial allocation of resources, be sent to the enemy, but fear and confusion on the home front must be quickly defeated. Because the Pearl Harbor attack was meant to dishearten Americans, Roosevelt's Declaration of War Address, Doolittle's raid and even the outpouring of troops to protect Alaska provided needed boosts to Americans' spirits. The elimination of fear and its replacement by the will to fight back and to make whatever sacrifices were necessary to win were the essential underpinnings of the response to the ultimate crisis.

But the cost was high. While the symbolic gesture of the Tokyo raid was purchased at relatively low cost, mobilization was not. The national budget and deficit ballooned beyond control, and, with the exception of Truman's efforts, no effort was made to reject programs on the grounds that they might be wasteful or unnecessary. Roosevelt required that, to respond forcefully to the Pearl Harbor attack, almost anything suggested, including the problematic Alcan projects, should be tried. Such a policy comes close to substituting panic for fear, not a healthy trade-off.

The American response was not only massive, but it had to be accomplished at top speed. Rapid mobilization is not merely a matter of putting people in uniform but also involves procurement of military materiel and civilian services. At the time of Pearl Harbor, the Government had not created a satisfactory mechanism for obtaining supplies or services to support the war effort. In fact, the initial impetus for the Truman Committee was the senator's realization that just a few, favored contractors, none of them in Missouri, were getting Government defense orders. The Government would turn to the largest enterprises, many with "dollar-a-year" men already on the ground in Washington, to take on defense production under cost-plus contracts under which they determined the costs, guaranteeing them large profits with little Government oversight. The Truman Committee barely dented this practice. Somervell's selection of Bechtel, already a major ship builder, to take on Canol was in line with normal practice. Bechtel had worked hard to position itself to profit when the Government needed help, and profit it did. Because of lack of a more reasonable standing policy that could be activated in time of crisis, such exorbitant profits or outright profiteering seemed to be an inevitable concomitant of the need for rapid mobilization.

Because the highest priority, in fact the only priority, in responding to surprise attack was to regain the initiative, commitment to that goal may have jeopardized many of the values that were being defended. This was the indirect cost of the crisis. Some of these sacrifices are thought to be temporary, but other costs may never be recovered. The construction of the Alcan Highway irrevocably undermined the way of life of thousands of natives in both Canada and Alaska and destroyed priceless environmental assets in the Canadian Northwest. Yet neither Canada nor the United States took these effects into account in making the hasty decision to proceed and, with the exception of the Kluane preserve, no prompt and preventive action was taken once Alcan had begun. Perhaps such costs were unavoidable; certainly no one cared about them as decisions were made. These were the eggs broken to make the Alcan omelet.

Once Alcan was launched, it gained momentum, making it impossible to stop and leading to ever-increasing costs. Despite its catastrophic failings in the build-up to Pearl Harbor, American intelligence about Japanese capabilities began to improve soon after the attack. The code breakers who understood that the invasion of the Aleutians was only a feint to draw forces away from Midway made possible just the kind of adjustment in strategy that allowed the best use of available forces. But information, based on direct observation as much as secret intelligence, showed that the Imperial Navy was incapable of anything more than harassment in the eastern Pacific, along the West Coast of North America. Supplies for Alaska and those used to support the road's construction flowed without interruption throughout 1942. Acting on this information, the Army could have left the Alcan Highway a pioneer road, and Canol could have been avoided. But these projects were never reassessed, the Army becoming defensive about any proposed cutbacks, even when it was no longer reasonable to proceed. Most of the Alcan projects' costs were incurred after December 1942, by which time intelligence had made evident that there was no need for the expenditures.

Finally, when the time came to account for what had been done and the huge sums that had been spent, military brass and the civilian leaders who had seemed anxious to meet the Army's every demand simply changed the justification for what they had done to cover for their weak judgment. Nowhere was that more obvious than in the attempt to justify the Alcan Highway as having been needed to guide Alsib pilots. Many aviators had flown the route safely well before the pioneer road was completed. Even if it had been a useful guide, it became no more of a guide with gravel on its surface than it had been as a dirt road. Even more egregious was the patently spurious claim that Canol was continued after it had been publicly ridiculed as a way of making Japanese intelligence believe that the United States might attack the home islands from the North. This unabashed rewriting of history in the immediate post-war world echoed in George Orwell's recounting of how history would be changed by a government's Ministry of Truth in his book *1984*, written in the late 1940s as even democratic governments rewrote World War II history.

The failure to halt Alcan when it was no longer necessary and the attempt to paper over history by changing the justification for it brought to an ignominious end an essential part of the American effort to tame the fear engendered by Pearl Harbor and to demonstrate the country's ability to mobilize.

The 9/11 Al Qaeda attacks showed that, as Roosevelt had said 60 years earlier, "our ocean-girt hemisphere is not immune from attack." The United States again faced the challenge of defending the homeland and suppressing fear.

As the history of the American response to the Al Qaeda attacks emerges, including the invasion and occupation of Iraq, we see remarkable parallels with the American answer to Pearl Harbor, as shown here by the Alcan experience, but undoubtedly not limited to it. Uncontrolled government, unlimited spending, runaway profits for war contractors, the suspension of basic American and democratic values and an ever-changing rationale, characteristics of the Pearl Harbor response, emerged again in a time of crisis. Perhaps such excesses are inevitable; they may be unavoidable unless some political leaders are willing to show the courage to urge moderation and reason in the face of a nation gripped by fear and seeking immediate action.

CHAPTER 15.

SUPERPOWERISM

On April 19, 1898, the day the Spanish-American War began, the United States became a world power. On December 7, 1941, the day American isolation ended, the United States became a superpower. On December 31, 1991, the day the Soviet Union ended, the United States became the only surviving superpower, the first time in its history that a single nation had been able to dominate world affairs.

Theodore Roosevelt, the Assistant Secretary of the Navy, inspired by the theories of naval strategist Alfred Thayer Mahan and with the strong support of Sen. Henry Cabot Lodge of Massachusetts, the leading foreign policy specialist in Congress, had managed to push the United States into war against Spain. Roosevelt believed that American greatness depended on its going to war: "No triumph of peace is quite so great as the supreme triumphs of war...."[372] He then set out, successfully, to argue, cajole and connive to get the United States into a war with Spain, a war that demonstrated to the world that the United States had arrived as a strong and independent force. Mahan, an armchair admiral, had theorized that Britain had ruled an empire by virtue of its naval strength and that the United States could play a similar role with the exercise of the same kind of maritime domination. Roosevelt put the theory into practice.

After the Spanish-American War ended, independence of action, championed by Roosevelt, became intertwined with the more innate isolationism of the American people. By the start of the World War I in 1913, President Woodrow

Wilson pitched his appeal to the nation's isolationist desire to stay out of the war, while Lodge, anxious to flex America's military muscle, argued for direct intervention. By the end of the war in which the United States had reluctantly participated, Wilson proposed that the League of Nations, a new international organization, should take over responsibility for maintaining the peace. Lodge, the first Harvard Ph.D. in political science and never an isolationist, successfully opposed American participation in the League because it might hinder America's freedom of action. His policy calling for an independent foreign policy could easily dissolve into isolationism, but Lodge did not suggest that the United States, a nascent superpower, should shrink from its role as one of arbiters of the world. His self-proclaimed "conservative" policy would simply assure it complete freedom of action. In his most well-known speech in opposition to the League of Nations, he said:

> I can never be anything else but an American, and I must think of the United States first, and when I think of the United States first in an arrangement like this I am thinking of what is best for the world, for if the United States fails, the best hopes of mankind fail with it.[373]

Both Lodge and Wilson saw the United States as a world leader. While Wilson believed that such leadership should be exercised within a multilateral organization, Lodge believed that what was good for the United States, acting alone, was good for the world, which would soon enough recognize that fact.

Lodge's conservative superpowerism served to defeat U.S. participation in the League, but the superpower itself rejected a leadership role as resurgent isolationism triumphed, not to end until Pearl Harbor pulled the United States back into world leadership. Franklin Roosevelt seized that opportunity both to advance American leadership and to insure that the United States would be bound to participate in a post-war coalition to keep the peace, by creating on January 1, 1942, the alliance he called the United Nations.

Its founding document required that all signatories accept the principles of the Atlantic Charter, adopted by the United States and Britain the previous August, which stated in part that: "... all of the Nations of the world, for realistic as well as spiritual reasons, must come to the abandonment of the use of force."[374] It called for "a wider and permanent system of general security ...." This declaration not only abandoned isolationism, but was a clean break with Theodore Roosevelt's glorification of war above peace and Lodge's conservative superpowerism that would not have tolerated a "permanent system of general security," the declared intent of the United Nations organization created in 1945.

Roosevelt placed the American war effort in a multilateral context for at least three reasons. First, he believed that isolationism had caused the United States to be insufficiently prepared for war and had forced it to the sidelines in the critical early stages of the war, a situation which could be prevented from recurring if the country were continuously engaged in maintaining the peace. Second, the United States could not win the war or keep the peace without joining with others. It shared common interests with Britain and its Dominions and with the countries of the Western Hemisphere. These allies had resources to contribute to help share the cost. And the United States, a former colony, abjured colonies and the acquisition of territory by force, so other countries' geography became part of their contribution to the alliance. Third, Roosevelt was worried about the postwar behavior of the Soviet Union and, by including it in his United Nations, he might hope to check its unilateral exercise of power.

Multilateralism was also an inducement for others to accept American leadership. Treaties and international organizations could provide mechanisms for limiting the unilateral exercise of American power. Nobody was more aware of that than Canada.

The American relationship with Canada, emerging from British rule with its own policies and interests, set the pattern for its relationship with all friendly countries once the

United States had irrevocably stepped forward as a super-power. While the two countries shared a wide range of common interests, Canada showed a continuous sensitivity to the protection of its sovereignty. To be sure, unlike other countries, sovereignty for Canada had a special meaning based on the need to protect its national territory from American incursions. But, like other countries, sovereignty for Canada also meant the need to preserve the ability to make decisions for itself and neither be dictated to nor run over by the United States.

In his relationship with Canada, as with other countries, Roosevelt understood the importance of intangibles in showing American respect for sovereign sensitivities.[375] As Canada became an increasingly important player, the American legation in Ottawa was upgraded to a full embassy. If Mackenzie King was miffed by his exclusion from Roosevelt's meeting with Churchill in Newfoundland waters, he was assuaged by being invited to negotiate with Roosevelt in the waters of the President's Hot Springs swimming pool. The ceremonial opening of the Alcan Highway, built entirely by Americans and partly in American territory, was a staunchly bilateral event.

Roosevelt's policy remained America's policy in the decades after the war. As the post-war world evolved into a struggle between the United States and the Soviet Union, the maintenance of a multilateral alliance was essential to American strategy. When the Soviet Union fell in December 1991, the notion of multilateralism survived, and the organization designed to protect against Soviet expansionism was opened to former adversaries. The United Nations itself, so often unable to act because of the fissures between the American-led West, the Soviet bloc and the Third World, moved toward greater effectiveness in maintaining peace. Multilateral arrangements grew more important as the world's desire for protection against possible unilateral action by the United States grew stronger. Just as Canada had protected itself by such mechanisms, the nations of the world, more nearly analogous to Canada in their dependence on the United States than ever before, relied on international structures.

Then came 9/11, a direct attack on the territory of the United States. No multilateral organization, no ally had served to prevent the attacks and protect the United States. The enemy was not a conventional member of the international community. The American government moved quickly toward a policy of independent international action against what it perceived as the sources of the threat to the United States, even if that meant acting unilaterally and no longer trying to assuage the ruffled feelings of allies in the White House swimming pool. Washington did not see military actions in Afghanistan and Iraq as traditional wars on nation-states; they were launched as wars against terrorists. These punitive assaults were taken by the United States and those nations willing to fall in behind it; terrorism had stripped away the use of a multilateral approach.

The unilateral response to 9/11 differed from the multilateral response to Pearl Harbor. President George W. Bush revived the spirit of Henry Cabot Lodge, declaring that "the course of this nation does not depend on the decisions of others. Whatever action is required, whenever action is necessary, I will defend the freedom and security of the American people."[376] He reiterated that "if we need to act we will act. And we really don't need the United Nations' approval to do so. ...when it comes to our security, we really don't need anybody's permission."[377] In the American view, the United Nations needed to be "relevant" — in agreement with American policy — or it was irrelevant and could be ignored.

Contrast the reaction of Canada in the two instances.

At the start of the Second World War, Canada worried openly about threats to its sovereignty by the United States. It acceded reluctantly to American requests to use its territory and resources about which it had valid doubts, because Roosevelt troubled to flatter and engage Canadian leaders and because the two countries shared a common

understanding of the threat. Canada made an enormous contribution to the war effort relative to its population.

In the immediate aftermath of 9/11, Canada again
moved immediately to the aid of the United States, despite
bruised feelings that the American government had stripped
it of its special position in international relations by a series
of heedless acts by the American President. Ultimately, the
United States proposed that Canadian armed forces in North
America should be placed under U.S. control, demonstrating a remarkable lack of sensitivity to Canadian sovereignty.

By the time that the American government was eagerly
seeking members for a "coalition of the willing" to pursue
the war in Iraq, Canada was not willing. The American government had become unhappy with Canada, and there
would be no stroking its sensitivities, as a columnist for the
Globe and Mail, noted:

> Those who run baseball from New York have
> ordered that God Bless America be played during
> the seventh-inning stretch of every game. That
> decree extended to Canada because no one bothered
> to consider how it might be viewed in this country,
> which isn't at war, where feelings about the conflict
> in Iraq are decidedly mixed ... and which remains a
> sovereign state."378

A "love-fear" relationship between the United States
and Canada had replaced, temporarily perhaps, the relationship first developed on the Alcan and other wartime
projects. Canadians openly expressed concern that they
would be the object of U.S. retaliation after the Iraq war
ended. One leader of a Canadian corporation with major
contracts in the United States, said "I am deeply, deeply
concerned about the deterioration of the U.S.-Canada relationship. ... I think if we are not careful, the standard of living of all Canadians could take quite a beating as a result of
this."379 Despite such concerns, Canada withheld its armed
forces from the new war effort, although people holding a
wide range of political perspectives in Canada believed that

their country no longer had much scope for indulging its sovereign prerogatives.[380]

The erosion of the relationship between the United States and Canada reflected the loss of much of the good will that had been built up in Ottawa over the years. The economic ties between the two countries were so great that the maintenance of the most friendly relations between the two had become a matter of necessity, especially for Canada. Yet the United States could not for long afford a policy of going it alone, especially if Canada and countries like it, France and Germany, for example, would insist on adopting their own policies even if they had to pay a price for it. Perhaps they would be willing to gamble that someday the United States might need them enough that it would tolerate their independence.

Senator Lodge's conservative policy in 1919 allowed for others to settle their own affairs, if they could do so without involving America's vital interests. But, by 2001, the world had changed to the point where virtually everything involves America's vital interests, and American actions affect the vital interests of almost all other countries. Even a superpower needs to remember both parts of this proposition.

NOTES

[1] "the Empire of Japan": Roosevelt, Franklin D., "Message to Congress Requesting a Declaration of War with Japan, December 8. 1941," *Public Papers of the Presidents, Franklin D. Roosevelt, 1941* at www.americanpresidency.org.

[2] "not immune from attack": Roosevelt, F.D., "Fireside Chat, December 9, 1941" in *Public Papers of the Presidents, 1941*.

[3] costly changes in its war strategy: Department of the Navy, Naval Historical Center, *Online Library of Selected Images* (www.history.navy.mil), Doolittle Raid on Japan, 18 April 1942.

[4] only 15,000 of its troops: Johnson, Gregory A., "Strategic Necessity or Military Blunder? Another Look at the Decision to Build the Alaska Highway" in *Three Northern Wartime Projects* (Edmonton, Canadian Circumpolar Institute, University of Alberta, 1996), 17.

[5] the most exposed position to attack: U.S. House of Representatives, Committee on Roads, *The Alaska Highway*, March 13, 1946, 9.

[6] Imperial Japanese Navy submarine fleet: Information on the Japanese submarine fleet from *Japanese Submarines at Pearl Harbor* at ww2pacific.com/japsubs.html.

[7] major shipping routes on the coast: Young, Donald J., "West Coast War Zone", *World War II* (magazine) at history1900s.about.com/library/prm/blwestcoastwarzone1.htm

[8] their response to Doolittle: Nobuo Fujita, the pilot, conceived of the mainland aerial attack. Under orders from Prince Takamatsu, the Emperor's younger brother and commander of the Japanese Imperial Navy, he was ordered to attempt to start forest fires in Oregon, which the Prince thought would cause great devastation. Fujita survived the war and later visited Oregon. Langenberg, William H., "Japanese Bomb the West Coast", from *Aviation History* magazine, November 1997, at history1900s.about.com/library/prm/bljapaneseplanesbombwc1/1.htm.

[9] had never sunk a vessel: Ames, Darrell D., "Determination Surfaces" in *World War II Submarines* at www.csp.navy.mil/centennial/prewar.htm

[10] twelve obsolete pursuit planes: Remley, David A., *Crooked Road* (New York, McGraw-Hill, 1976), 128-129

[11] "what I've got to do up there": U.S. House of Representatives, Committee on Roads, *op. cit.*, 9

[12] the huge area of the territory: *Ibid.*

[13] its hold on occupied areas: See Prange, G.W., *At Dawn We Slept* (New York, McGraw-Hill, 1981), passim.

[14] projected raid on Wake Island: *Japanese Submarines at Pearl Harbor.*

[15] come up with the needed funds: Johnson, *op. cit.*, 7

[16] actual construction in Alaska: Remley, *op. cit.*, 121.

[17]recommended a highway: U.S. House of Representatives, Committee on Roads, *op. cit.*,6.

[18]British Columbia by itself: Remley, *op. cit.*, 121-2.

[19]"the possibility of any construction": Johnson, *op. cit.*, 9 includes the quotes from Mackenzie King's notes.

[20]most passionate advocates of the road: Johnson, *op. cit.*,10.

[21]a federal appointment: Twichell, Heath, *Northwest Epic* (New York, St. Martin's Press, 1992). Gruening would later serve as one of the first two elected U.S. senators from Alaska.

[22]service for six months: Johnson, *op. cit.*, 11. and Coates, Ken, *North to Alaska!* (Toronto, McClelland & Stewart, 1992), 24-25.

[23]tourists expected to follow: For a description of each of the routes, see Twichell, *op. cit.*, 12-26.

[24]issued a favorable report: U.S. House of Representatives, Committee on Roads, *op. cit.*, 6.

[25]"defense measure was negligible": Remley, *op. cit.*, 120, based on National Archives, DLFB, BB, files A204[2].

[26]"against the North American continent": Johnson, *op. cit.*, 14, quoting *Documents on Canadian External Relations (DCER)*, vol. III, no. 280, 454-6, Military Appreciation of the General Staff, 2 November 1940.

[27]dominate the Pacific: Johnson, *op. cit.*, 14, from Conn, Engleman, and Fairchild, *Guarding the United States and Its Outposts* (Washington, U.S. Army, Center of Military History, 1964), 340.

[28]"such as aviation fields": Johnson, *op. cit.*, 15, from Conn and Fairchild, *Framework of Hemisphere Defense* (Washington, U.S. Army, Center of Military History, 1960), 392.

[29]"by the Washington Government": Cohen, Stanley, *The Trail of 42* (Missoula, Pictorial Histories, Publishing, 1979), 2. Apparently the Americans had held off telling the Canadians about this article for fear they would misunderstand it.

[30]"long range defense measure": Committee on Roads, *op. cit.*, 8.

[31]"low priority": Bezeau, M.V., "The Decision to Build the Alaska Highway," in Coates, Kenneth, ed. *The Alaska Highway: Papers of the 40th Anniversary Symposium* (Vancouver, University of British Columbia Press,1985), 27.

[32]the winter operating conditions: Johnson, *op. cit.*, 18 and Remley, *op. cit.*, 128.

[33]"our clever and determined enemy": Johnson, *op. cit.*,19, quoting from FDR Papers, PSF, Box 1, Safe File: Alaska, Office of Chief of Naval Operations, *Memorandum for Roosevelt*, 14 January 1942.

[34]"possibly critical importance": Remley, *op. cit.*, 238-239, quoting *Hampton to the Secretary of the Interior*, 14 January 1942 (NA, SERD, 9-1-55, box 372).

[35]"equivocal and unsatisfactory": Dzubian, Stanley W., *Military Relations Between the United States and Canada* (Washington, U.S. Army, Center of Military History, 1990), *1939-1945*, 218 (both quotes). Dzubian's book is the officially sanctioned Army view of events.

[36]"more pressing National Defense undertakings": Remley, *op. cit.*,131.

[37]offset the obvious drawbacks: Bezeau, *op. cit.*, 29

[38]just two days later: *Ibid.*

[39]"uninterrupted communications": Bezeau, *op. cit.*, 29-30.

[40]"a long time to die": Johnson, *op.cit.*, 17, quoting from Dower, John, *War Without Mercy*, 112.

[41]force Roosevelt to negotiate with them: Johnson, *op.cit.*, 24, from Stephan, John J., *Hawaii Under the Rising Sun*, 85, 89-109, 169 and Wilmott, H.P., *The Barrier and the Javelin*, 82ff.

[42]"for future assault operations":Johnson, *op.cit.*, 24-25 from PRO, War Office Records, WO 208/956. Intelligence Memorandum No. 8, G-2 Section, 3 August 1943.

[43]"against our West Coast": *Canol*, War Department Misc. 957, 1944 (film).

[44]wrote one analyst in 1992: Johnson, *op.cit.*, 17.

[45]British, French or American: Perhaps the definitive work on the differences between the United States and Canada is Lipset, Seymour Martin, *Continental Divide* (New York, Routledge, 1990). In my own extensive business and personal relationships with Canada and Canadians, I have reached much the same conclusions as he did, although I have found Canadians who disagree.

[46]"social conformity": Lipset, 54, citing Neatby H. Blair, *The Politics of Chaos: Canada in the Thirties*, 10-14 reporting on Angus, ed., *Canada and her Great Neighbor*, 392-438.

[47]protected Canada against aggression: Dziuban, 2.

[48]outnumbered by more than 11-to-1: Based on the 1940 U.S. census and the 1941 Canadian census. Mexico was not yet considered to be part of North America.

[49]Britain somewhat at bay: Canada established its own diplomatic relations with the United States only in the 1920s.

[50]"close to each other": Maddox, W.P., "Canadian-American Defense Planning," *Foreign Policy Association Report*, XVII, No. 17 (November 15, 1941), 220.

[51]hit the same note: Remley, David, "The Latent Fear: Canadian-American Relations and Early Proposals for a Highway to Alaska" in Coates, Kenneth, ed., *The Alaska Highway: Papers of the 40th Anniversary Symposium*, 2.

[52]"financial penetration": Johnson, Gregory A., "Strategic Necessity or Military Blunder?" in Hesketh, Bob, ed., *Three Northern Wartime Projects*, 11 quoting King papers, vol. 171, file 1594, c121644-48, King minute on Skelton Memorandum, 26 April 1938.

[53]appropriated the Panama Canal: Twichell, 18.

[54]sparsely populated areas of the country: Johnson, Gregory A., 10-11 and Fisher, Robin, "T.D.Pattullo and the British Columbia to Alaska Highway", in Coates, *The Alaska Highway*, 17-18.

[55]"one its major justifications":Remley, "The Latent Fear," 6, quoting Memorandum to Secretary Burlew, 4 August 1938, NA SERD, Box 372, file 9-1-55.

[56]"masters in our own house": Remley, David, "The Latent Fear", 7, quoting Hutchins articles in the Vancouver *Sun* of January 31, 1939 and May 9, 1939, both of which affirmed that the U.S. military was not interested in the road.

[57]"defend our neighborhood": Dziuban, 3, quoting Department of State, *Press Releases*, XV, 168.

[58]"by any other empire": Dziuban, 4, quoting Department of State, *Press Releases*, XIX, 124.

[59]Roosevelt's own handwriting: Dziuban, 4, quoting Hull, Cordell, *The Memoirs of Cordell Hull*, I, 587-588.

[60]"across Canadian territory":Dziuban, 4, quoting *House of Common Debates*, November 12, 1940, 55.

[61]outbreak of war in September 1939: Dziuban, 4.

[62]could to help Britain: In fact, Mackenzie King felt the U.S. relationship should be given priority, while his generals favored Britain.

[63]subject to German interference: Stacey, C.P., *Arms, Men and Governments* (Ottawa, Queen's Printer, 1970), 330, quoting official sources. Stacey wrote this official history of the Department of National Defence.

[64]United States abandoned its neutrality: Stacey, 330-331

[65]"alarming and distressing": Stacey, 331.

[66]territories in the Western hemisphere: Dziuban, 19. This group favored support for the British, but was divided on the issue of American intervention. It clashed with isolationist groups like America First, supported by Charles Lindbergh, who though Britain was doomed, and the American automobile manufacturers having large German investments. On August 4, 1940, General John J. Pershing, the American military leader in World War I, made a national broadcast supporting the Century Group position. See vanden Heuvel, William J., *Address to the Monthly Meeting of the Century Association*, April 4, 2002.

[67]"improved overnight": Stacey, 334.

[68]"defence of the Pacific": Johnson, 18, quoting *DCER*, vol. VIII, no. 276, 451, Skelton to King, July 20, 1940.

[69]"its strategic value": Johnson, 18, quoting *DCER*, vol VIII, no. 279, 453, Keenleyside Memorandum, "The Pacific Coast," August 17, 1940.

[70]"some diplomacies fail": Stacey, 336. Previously Roosevelt had tried to get Mackenzie King to agree to make the proposal to move the fleet across the Atlantic seem to come from him rather than the Americans. Mackenzie King also demurred then. Emphasis in the original.

[71]would have equal weight: Dziuban, 26.

[72]"feel on this subject": Stacey, 338-339, quoting Stimson Diary.

[73]should be "permanent": It still exists.

[74]what had been accomplished: Stacey, 341.

[75]funded by the Canadians in December: Dziuban, 201-202.

[76]truly cooperative basis by the two government: Dziuban, 200. See below chapter on ALSIB.

[77]extension of Ogdensburg: The Hyde Park Declaration is found in Dziuban, Appendix D, 373.

[78]"any infatuated swain": MacDonald, Malcolm, "Report to the Dominions Office on Hyde Park Agreement, 24 April 1941" in Grant, Shelagh, *Sovereignty or Security* (Vancouver, University of British Columbia Press, 1988), Appendix D, 259-260.

[79]LaGuardia favored it: Dziuban, 218

[80]until January 1, 1944: Dziuban, 219.

[81]"is not warranted": Stacey, 382, quoting H.Q.C. 631-52-1, vol. 1.

[82]"a terrific political backfire": Dziubin, 220, n.60 and Conn, Stetson and Fairchild, Byron, *The Framework of Hemisphere Defense*, 394-395, quoting Letter, LaGuardia to President, 27 February 1942, Roosevelt Papers, FDRL.

[83]"for reasons of general policy": Dziuban, 219, quoting Keenleyside MS; Memo/Conv, Moffat and Hickerson, 7 Feb 42, and Moffat and Robertson, 6 Mar 42, Moffat Diary.

[84]Canada must acquiesce: The Canadian military may have also become more uneasy about the possibility of Japanese attacks after the fall of Singapore and the destruction of the British Pacific fleet. Johnson, 24.

[85]"friends learn of the route": Tynan, T.M., *The Role of the Arctic in Canadian-American Relations* (unpublished dissertation, Washington, The Catholic University, 1976), 156.

[86]plan was not to be changed: For a detailed discussion of the opposition to the route, especially by Senator William Langer of North Dakota, see Twichell, ch. 5.

[87]"the whole of the Western Hemisphere": Johnson, 22, quoting *King Papers*, diary, March 21, 1942.

[88]the provision was dropped: Dziuban, 221.

[89]sensitivity about its sovereignty: Conn and Fairchild, 395-396.

[90]of only 150 aircraft: Smith, Blake W., *Warplanes to Alaska* (Surry, B.C., Hancock House, 1998), 18.

[91]the U.S. would provide aid: Hays, Otis, Jr., *The Alaska-Siberia Connection* (College Station, Texas A&M University Press, 1996), 15-16.

[92]"reference to the Devil": Colville, John, *Fringes of Power* (New York, W.W. Norton, 1985), 406. Colville was a member of Churchill's staff.

[93]excellent condition, he said: Hays, 16.

[94]training on U.S. bombers: Hays, 17-18.

[95]should travel by ship: Hays 21.

[96]"result in indeterminate delays": Hays, 25, quoting from *Deane Report* October 18, 1943-October 31, 1945, NA RG 334 71/107.

[97]"weather reporting and communications facilities": Hays, 25.

[98]"assistance to the Soviet Union": Hays, 29, quoting Lukas, Richard C., *Eagles East: The Army Air Force and the Soviet Union*, 105.

[99]"assigned to Soviet airmen": Hays 29, quoting Mazurek, "Alaska-Siberia Airlift," *Soviet Life* (Oct. 1979), 30.

[100]although primitive, could be used: Hays, 29-31.

[101]North Sea to Murmansk: Smith, 27-28.

[102]full-scale U.S. participation: Jenkins, Roy, *Churchill* (Farrar, Straus and Giroux, 2001), 667.

[103]"threatened in the autumn": Stacey, C.P., *Arms, Men and Government*, 37.

[104]"won after all": Churchill, Winston S., *Second World War, III* (Boston, Houghton Mifflin, 1950), 539

[105]."Emperor of the East": Jenkins, 676. The proof of U.S. control was the appointment, at General Marshall's suggestion of British General Archibald Wavell to command the south-west Pacific area. Churchill did not think highly of Wavell. When he communicated with Wavell in January 1942, he noted that only Washington and not he could send him instructions. See Jenkins, 677.

[106]as three years earlier: Conn, Stetson, *Highlights of Mobilization, World War II, 1938-1942* (ms. in U.S. Army, Center of Military History, 10 March 1959, File 2-3.7 AF.B).

[107]"the rest of humanity": Roosevelt, F.D., "Message to Congress Requesting a Declaration of War with Japan."

[108]41 percent were black: U.S. House of Representatives, Committee on Roads, *The Alaska Highway*, 104-105. Actually, the total number included other Engineer, Signal and Quartermaster units, some of which had black soldiers. The share of black soldiers in the seven regiments themselves was 42 percent. Almost all blacks were enlisted personnel; the five black chaplains were the only black officers.

[109]served in the revolutionary army: Dalfiume, Richard M., *Desegregation of the U.S. Armed Forces* (Columbia, University of Missouri Press, 1969), 5.

[110]issued the Emancipation Proclamation: Dalfiume, 6.

[111]"Lord Acton's famous dictum": Morris, Edmund, *Theodore Rex* (New York, Random House, 2001), 554.

[112]"provoke race animosity": Dalfiume, 13, quoting Scott, *The American Negro in the World War*, 97-98.

[113]"this division to be a failure": "The Negro and the War Department," *The Crisis*, XVI (May 1918), 7-8.

[114]commend the black troops: Dalfiume, 16.

[115]"they are hopelessly inferior": Dalfiume, 15.

[116]"its largest minority": Dalfiume, 20.

[117]"soldiers still in uniform": Dalfiume 20.

[118]"rising negro population, nothing": Lee, Ulysses, *The Employment of Negro Troops* (Washington, U.S. Army Center of Military History, 2001), 32, quoting Memo G-3 for CofC, 28 Nov 22, AG 322.97 (11-18-22) (1). The 34 percent was based on British losses in World War I.

[119]"marked sense of rhythm": Lee, 45, quoting Army War College study, 1936.

[120]"modern civil rights movement": MacGregor, Morris J., Jr., *Integration of the Armed Forces 1940-1965* (Washington, U.S. Army, Center of Military History, 2001), 9.

[121]"to the white race": Lee, 73.

[122]"approximately 10 percent": Lee 75.

[123]"now under consideration": Lee, 75.

[124]Plessy v. Ferguson: 167 U.S. 357 (1896) No. 210.

[125]toward fully unsegregated units: MacGregor, 15. For the text of the memo presented by the black leaders, see, Lee, 74-75.

[126]to lead black units: Lee, 75-76 for the text of the policy statement.

[127]"the election will be over": Lee, 79-80, quoting *Time*, November 4, 1940, 20.

[128]"the colored Admiral": McGuire, Phillip, ed., *Taps for a Jim Crow Army* (Lexington, The University Press of Kentucky, 1983), xxxi-xxxii, quoting Stimson diary, October 22, 25, 1940.

[129]"all branches of the military service": Lee, 80, quoting *Letter, SW to Dean William H. Hastie*, 25 October 1940, OAS Personnel #301.

[130]"jurisdiction of the War Department": Lee, 81, quoting *Memo, Civ Aide for USW*, 7 Feb 41, AG 322.97 (3-18-41) (1).

[131]"concurrence before final action": Lee, 81, quoting *Ltr, TAG to Chief Arms and Svcs and Divs of WD Gen Staff*, 18 Dec 40, AG 291.21 (12-17-40) M-OCS-M.

[132]about the military: Dalfiume, 117-121.

[133]"brawn is a prerequisite": Lee, 146-147, quoting *Draft Ltr, TAG to Brig. Gen L.D. Gasser, WD Representative OCD*, 2 Sept 41 in Memo G-1 for Col. Boyer (AGO), 3 Sep 41, AG 291.21 (9-4-41) (1).

[134]"some place in the armed services": Lee, 136-139. Both quotes from *Survey and Recommendations Concerning the Integration of the Negro Soldier into the Army.* Memo Civ Aide to SW for SW through USW, 22 Sep 41, G-1/15640-120.

[135]"efficiency, discipline and morale": Lee, 140-141, quoting *Memo CofS for SW*, 1 Dec 41, OCS 20602-219.

[136]"satisfied with it either": Lee, 142.

[137]"solution of their problems": Lee, 142, quoting *Speech, The Adjutant General's Department*, AG 291.21 (12-1-41) (1).

[138]"given combat training": Dalfiume, 59, quoting *Memo, Hastie to Undersecretary of War Patterson*, February 5, 1942, ASW 291.2, NARG 335.

[139]compared with combat units: Lee, 134.

[140]there were 97,725: Lee, 88.

[141]would be 467,883 black troops: Lee, 134.

[142]In the Army Engineers, platoons form into companies, companies into battalions, battalions into regiments. Regiments may become part of a brigade or, in the case of the Alcan, into a Command. Frequently, Engineer regiments would be part of larger combat units.

[143]skill than those of a laborer: Lee, 94.

[144]work on the Alcan Highway began: Lee, 128-129.

[145]20 percent of whites agreed: *American Soldier Survey, Attitudes of and Toward Negroes*, AMS-032N, AMS-032W, March 1943. The Army produced scores of surveys continuously throughout the war. This survey was conducted in Birmingham, Raleigh, Oklahoma City, Chicago and Detroit.

[146]service overseas: "Overseas" meant outside of the 48 states, so that what would today be called foreign duty included Hawaii and Alaska, and Canada seems to have been considered in part domestic and in part foreign.

[147]unacceptable aspirations among the natives: Among such places were the British Caribbean and the Belgian Congo.

[148]"No, don't yield": Lee, 430, quoting *Memo WPD for CofS*, 25 Mar 42, OPD 291.2 with handwritten and initialed notes from Stimson.

[149]78 percent of blacks opposed it: *The American Soldier*, AMS-03SN/W, 46

[150]"ungenerous and unchivalrous": *Correspondence Between Ulysses S. Grant and Simon B. Buckner Discussing Surrender Terms at Fort Donelson*, www.civilwarhome/grant-don.htm.

[151]"Canadians also prefer whites": NA 52 A 434, box 30, file 611, Alcan Highway, C.L. Sturdevant to S.B. Buckner, 2 Apr 1942. Cited in Morgan, Lael, "Remembering Black Troops who Built the Alcan" in Hesketh, R., 151.

[152]"racial problems here and elsewhere": S.B. Buckner to C.L. Sturdevant, April 20, 1942, NA RG 77, OCE, Box 14/20, Alaska Highway.

[153]the use of black troops: The Army found that Canada and Newfoundland "recognize the necessity for us to send United States troops, regardless of color, to their territory" and

would not create serious difficulties. Memo, OPD for G-2, 6 Jun 42, OPD 291.21/9, cited in Lee, 435. The Canadian Chief of Staff was reported to have complained informally about black anti-aircraft troops being stationed near Sault Ste. Marie, but backed down. Lee, 439.

[154]"cultural background": Lee, 242.

[155]"about native intelligence": Lee, 242, quoting Bingham, Walter V. in Caliver, Ambrose, ed., *Post War Education of Negroes*, 25.

[156]results for blacks did not: Lee, 246, citing Bingham, Walter V., "Personnel Classification testing in the Army," *Science*, C (Sept. 29, 1944), 276.

[157]Table 2. Lee, 244, from Tab A, Memo G-3 for CofS, 10 Apr 43, AG 201.6 (19 Mar 43) (1),

[158]widely different educational backgrounds: U.S. Army, Special Services Branch, Research Division, *Some New Statistics on the Negro Enlisted Man*, Report No. 2, February 17, 1942, 4. NA.

[159]67 percent in the North: *The American Soldier*, AMS-03SN/W, 28.

[160]"a damn with colored troops": Lee, 255.

[161]"loyalty is not the least of these": Lee, 255.

[162]"command hierarchy of the U.S. Army": Twichell, 132.

[163]."when the unit moved:" Telephone interview with Jesse Balthazar, October 2, 2002.

[164]near the Alaska border: Set at Snag, Yukon, February 3, 1947.

[165]could not stand the cold as well as whites: Lee, 291-292.

[166]"built by black labor": Lee, 430.

[167] stereotyping by climate was nothing new: Morris, *Theodore Rex*, 468.

[168]."did not suffer much exposure": Medical Department, United States Army, *Cold Injury, Ground Type*, 379-380. But the report says that two later studies, one in Korea and the other in Europe, indicate that "race is a predisposing factor" in frostbite, although the evidence may be anecdotal and not sufficient to support the conclusion.

[169]"coldest imaginable temperatures": Neuberger, Richard L, "Yukon Adventure," *Saturday Evening Post*, February 19, 1944. Reprinted in Congressional Record, House of Representatives, March 2, 1944, 172-173.

[170]"as well as anyone else": Boyd Robert Platt, Jr., *Me and Company "C"* (self-published, 1992),,, 79.

[171]"small fraction of summer efficiency": Lee, 439, quoting *Rpt of Inspection of QM Activities of Alaska and Northwestern Canada*, 9 Dec 42 to 25 Jun 43, OQMG R&D Br Reading File.

[172]virtual isolation from others: See Gawande, Atul, "Cold Comfort," *The New Yorker*, March 11, 2002, 42-47 reporting on studies revealing that no reason for the spread of colds has been determined.

[173]"all diseases was astonishing": NA RG 112 Entry 54A, Box 235.

[174]slow, venal and subservient: The actor's real name was Lincoln Perry, reputedly a quite intelligent person, but he was despised by many blacks for playing the role.

[175]"sapped the strength" of their victims: Breedon, James O., "Disease as a Factor in Southern Distinctiveness," in Savitt, T.L. and Young, J.H.,eds., *Disease and Distinctiveness in the American South* (Knoxville, University of Tennessee Press, 1988), 11-12.

[176]."native foreigners" in their own country: Marcus, Alan I., "The South's Native Foreigners; Hookworm as a Factor in Southern Distinctiveness," in Savitt and Young, 79-99.

[177]"the morale of Negro troops is low;" Morale Services Division, Alaskan Department, "What Soldiers in Alaska Think," *Attitudes of Negro Soldiers*, August 1944, 17. NA.

[178]"low in spirits": Research Branch, Central Pacific Base Command, *Attitudes of Negro Troops*, November 1944, 4. NA

[179]"no Service Clubs for blacks": Interview with Nehemiah Atkinson, October 7, 2002.

[180]the same buildings as whites: Research Branch, War Department, *Attitudes of White Enlisted Men Toward Sharing Facilities with Negro Troops*, July 30, 1942, 3. NA

[181]"nice guys though": Broadfoot, Barry, ed., *Six War Years 1939-1945: Memories of Canadians at Home and Abroad* (Toronto, Doubleday Canada, 1974) 220.

[182]"attitude would be short lived": *Alaska Command, Weekly Intelligence Report, 24 April 1943*. NA RG 407 Entry 427 Box 7.

[183]"resembling their natural habitat": *Alaska Command, Weekly Intelligence Report, 8 May 1943* (both quotes). See note 36.

[184]"and they were miserable": Broadfoot, 217.

[185]"everybody kicked them around": Broadfoot, 222.

[186]"leadership in many units was therefore deficient": Lee, 188.

[187]not doing better in training: Lee, 185.

[188]."hard guys": Interview with Joseph Haskin, October 1, 2002.

[189]"convert them into fertilizer": Twichell, 178-179, quoting censored mail NA RG 77 OCE, Box 15/20, Folder 50-26.

[190]"boy really meant it": Ibid. (both quotes)

[191]took on leadership roles: Boyd, 47-48.

[192]"attempt to kiss": *Memo P.C. Pack, Judge Advocate to Chief of Staff, NWSC*, April 20, 1943. NA RG 338 Entry: NWSC. Box 1.

[193]"quickly shipped out": Interview with James Lancaster, October 15, 2002.

[194]"in the name of military efficiency": MacGregor, 38-39.

[195]"Harvest of Disorder": Lee, 348-379.

[196]"Mileage Under Construction": House of Representatives, Committee on Roads, 15.

[197]"than the white regiments": Heath Twichell interview, February 10, 2003.

[198]"failsafe missions he gave them": Twichell, 146.

[199]"perceptions of blacks at the time": Twichell interview.

[200]kept reasonably isolated: Twichell, 146.

[201]trailing along behind it: Twichell, 180-181.

[202]credit for their part: For example, Morgan, Lael, 150, wrote that the Corps of Engineers official history gives them one footnote. She referred to the CE study of the war on Japan, but the CE historians actually considered the Alcan as part of the defense of the continental United States, where their history contains liberal references to the black troops, including one the most famous photos of their involvement, Sims shaking hands with Jafulka.

[203].Lee, 609.

[204]"They inhale deeply": Rosten, Norman, *The Big Road* (New York, Rinehart, 1946), 228.

[205]"practically useless": Hoge, William M. Interview transcript, Jan. 14-15/April 15-17, 1974. Tape 2, 21 as quoted in Twichell, 145.

[206]"physical capacity of the troops": Letter of instruction from Sturdevant to Hoge, quoted in Twichell, 68.

[207]"completion of the project": U.S. House of Representatives, Committee on Roads, 13.

[208]stretch of the road to build: Greenwood, John T., "Building the Road to Alaska," in Fowles, Barry W., *Builders and Fighters: U.S. Army Engineers in World War II* (Washington, U.S. Government Printing Office, 1993), 120-122.

[209]continued for months: Twichell, 115-116.

[210]"Hoge has to go": Twichell, 205, quoting Minutes, HQSOS, August 24, 1942. See also Greenwood, "General Bill Hoge and the Alaska Highway," *The Alaska Highway*, Coates, K., ed., 39-53.

[211]responsibility for the Alcan Highway: Twichell, 206.

[212]Attu, Kiska and Adak: The Aleutian occupation was widely reported at the time but forgotten later. A good account with many photos is provided in Cohen, Stan, *The Forgotten War* (Missoula, Pictorial Histories Publishing, 1981), Vol. 1, especially 126-211.

[213]"construction of the Panama Canal": Rainey, 143.

[214]"spirit of the American soldier": Northwest Service Command, *History of the Whitehorse Sector of the Alcan Highway*. NA RG 404, Box 427/31.

[215]"there is no precedent": U.S. House of Representatives, Committee on Roads, 12.

[216]response to such an attack: More detail is provided by Twichell, 28-32.

[217]trip to Nome, Alaska: Mitchel Field was named in 1918 for a former New York City reform mayor who had died while flying an Army plane. Its name had nothing to with Gen. Mitchell, for whom the Milwaukee airport is named.

[218]interest in the United States remained low: Hays, 11-12, and Smith, Blake W., *Warplanes to Alaska*, 31.

[219]Watson Lake and Whitehorse: Stacey, 379-380, and Dziuban, 201.

[220]"earliest possible date by Canada": Dziuban, 351. Also the quotes below from the Tenth Recommendation of the PJBD.

[221]the generator was repaired: Smith, 42-43.

[222]over the NWSR: Smith, 46-47.

[223]combat flying against the Japanese: Smith, 52-54.

[224]commercial planes for transport duty: Dziuban, 204.

[225]"the job we were assigned": Smith, 146, quoting pilot Carl H. Biron.

[226]in ever-increasing amounts: Dziuban, 216-217.

[227]first been requested: Hays, 44-45.

[228]loss of 112 lives: Hays, Appendix A, and Twichell, 287. In the U.S. itself. 74 planes had been lost en route to Grand Falls.

[229]never solved: Hays, 82-84.

[230]developing the atomic bomb: Smith, 141-144.

[231]trainers were also sent: Data on planes sent to the Soviet Union from Hays, 56, 86, 131, Appendix A.

[232]use in Alaska: Dziuban, 216.

[233]"made that impossible now": Smith, 247.

[234]Northwest gradually complied: Dziuban, 308-310.

[235]work at two airfields: Stacey, 380-381.

[236]under U.S. control: Recommendations 31 and 32 in Dziuban, 361-364.

[237]shelling from German U-boats: Dziuban, 228.

[238]"at the earliest practicable date": Twichell, 156 from *ASF, CD Report on Canol Project, 1 June 1945*, Office of History of the Corps of Engineers, 44-46. (Canol Report.)

[239]"the number of his enemies": Twichell, 161.

[240]"the cost and effort": Truman Committee, *Hearings*, Pat. 22, 9596.

[241]"has my full approval": Twichell, 162 quoting Canol Report, which may be considered to be of uncertain accuracy.

[242]as far as the Aleutians: Twichell, 195.

[243]"we had tails": Interview with Frank Brehon, November 24, 2002.

[244]shooting craps: Canol (film).

[245]"Canadians in the area": Department of External Affairs Records, External Affairs Archives, file 4349-40C, Hugh Keenleyside to Norman Robertson, 6 October 1942, quoted in Diubaldo, Richard J., "The Canol Project in Canadian-American Relations," *Historical Papers*, The Canadian Historical Association, 1977, 183.

[246]"complete ignorance": Ibid., Cotrelle to Norman Robertson, 28 September 1942, in Diubaldo, 183.

[247]approved by both governments: PJBD, *Twenty-Eighth Recommendation*, January 13, 1943, in Dziuban, 358-359.

[248]256,358 of diesel: Twichell, 273.

[249]"certainly not": Roosevelt, F.D., Press Conference, February 17, 1942, *Public Papers of the Presidents, 1942.*

[250]urging more joint effort: Roosevelt, F.D., Address to the Canadian People, *Public Papers of the Presidents, 1942.*

[251]"will do, if anything": Roosevelt, Press Conference, February 17, 1942, *Public Papers of the Presidents, 1942.*

[252]the date of the attack: www.worldwar2history.info/Midway/ambush.html.

[253]"end of the beginning": quoted in Jenkins, 702.

[254]"contractor's dream": Coates, Ken, *North to Alaska*, 145.

[255]"entire length of the highway": Committee on Roads, 51.

[256]60,000 tons a year: Committee on Roads, 51-52.

[257]Alaska without the NWSR: Dziuban, 216.

[258]fulfilled their principal role: Conn and Fairchild, 398.

[259]the reason for its routing: Committee on Roads, ix.

[260]"under certain conditions": Roosevelt, Press Conference, February 17, 1942, *Public Papers of the Presidents, 1942.*

[261]"many years to come": Quoting in Grant, 75. She believes that this was the only reason for the road.

[262]construction of Fort Leonard Wood: McCullough, David, *Truman* (New York, Simon and Schuster, 1992), 256.

[263]Senate Appropriations Committee: Riddle, Donald H., *The Truman Committee* (New Brunswick, Rutgers University Press, 1964), 12. This book is the most complete study of the Committee.

[264]"investigation on my own": Truman, Harry S, *Memoirs* (Garden City, Doubleday, 1955), I, 165.

[265]located in the East: McCullough, 256.

[266]"smaller than Missouri": Truman, 166.

[267]"their former companies": Truman, 183. Emphasis in the original.

[268]understood or simply patronized: McCullough, 257.

[269]awarding of defense contracts: S. Res. 71, introduced February 13, 1941.

[270]Lincoln and his generals: Riddle, 6.

[271]than did the Army: McCullough, 257.

[272]"the committee deems appropriate," Riddle 15, quoting S. Res. 71, March 1, 1941. This was the ninth of the Committee's mandates.

[273]"unspectacular competence": McCullough, 259.

[274]"take it for the truth": McCullough, 226,

[275]to head his staff: McCullough, 259

[276]money could not be saved: McCullough, 262 (both quotations).

[277]"Speed, speed, speed": McCullough, 257

[278]"dynamite in a Tiffany box": Twichell, 258.

[279]"stepping on his toes": McCullough, 262.

[280]"He went ahead anyway": McCullough, 262.

[281]"whatever they might be": Riddle, 110-111.

[282]"immediately stopped": Riddle, 111.

[283]"necessary to the war effort": Riddle, 112.

[284]"scrupulously honest": McCullough, 285.

[285]on the list: McCullough, 286.

[286]"prevent our trial": NA RG 338, NWSC Entry, Box 71.

[287]"double the size of the installation": NA RG 160, Entry 1, Box 4, Somervell Memorandum to Gen. Peckham, November 10, 1943.

[288]"man-hours and materials together": Riddle, 114.

[289]"defense of the Northwest": NA RG 160, Entry 1, Box 4, Franklin D. Roosevelt, *Press Statement*, December 28, 1943.

[290]"given his approval": the only authority indicating that he had approved of Canol was Somervell.

[291]"repeated warnings is inexcusable": U.S. Senate, Special Committee to Investigate the National Defense Program [Truman Committee], *The Canol Project*, January 8, 1944, 460.

[292]"equitable contract from Canada": *Op. cit.*, 458.

[293]"take advantage of the United States": *Op. cit.*, 480.

[294]"attention of the War Department": *Op. cit.*, 461.

[295]"the highway was finished": *Op. cit.*, 484-485.

[296]"performance of General Somervell": *The New York Times*, January 9, 1943, 17. The official Army study of the Army Service Forces showed that Patterson actually worked for Somervell, and civilian control of the military in this area was mostly myth.

[297]"one fly speck": NA RG 160, Entry 1, Box 4, Transcript of telephone conversation between High Fulton and Col. Knowles, July 25, 1944.

[298]"sympathetic to your needs": Somervell, Brehon B., "Concurrent Planning by Industry," November 17, 1948, 5.

[299]"may have had some justification": Millett, John D., *The Organization and Role of the Army Service Forces* (Washington, U.S. Army, Center of Military History, 1954), 395.

[300]"big enough to admit it": Fulton-Knowles, July 25, 1944. NA RG 160, Entry 1, Box 4.

[301]who had seen the files of the Joint Production Survey Committee: *The New York Times*, "Canol Plan Held Move to Fool Foe," October 8, 1946, 3.

[302]"digging up of dead horses": Harry S Truman, News Conference of September 5, 1946, Question 3, *Public Papers of the Presidents, 1946.*

[303]"plan to fool the enemy": *The New York Times*, October 8, 1946, 3.

[304]attack from the North: Millett, 394.

[305]"expenditure in foreign countries": Quoted in Grant, S.D., 130.

[306]price cuts a victory: *The New York Times*, "Canol Oil Prices Sharply Reduced," May 6, 1944, 17.

[307]."pre-Canol status": *The New York Times*, "'Canol' A Problem in Post-War Era," November 28, 1943, 31 .

[308]percentage of the costs as profits: McCartney, 66

[309]civil actions against the firms: NA RG 407, Entry 427, Box 32, Alaska Defense Command, Intelligence Report, April 15, 1944.

[310]"upsetting reading for Roosevelt": Brinkley, David, *Washington Goes to War* (New York, Knopf, 1988), 66.

[311]acknowledged Truman's objectivity: Riddle, 159-169, citing *Congressional Record*, August 14, 1941, 7117-7118.

[312]seven in 1943: Coates, K.S. and Morrison, W.R., *The Alaska Highway in World War II: The U.S. Army of Occupation in Canada's Northwest* (Norman, University of Oklahoma Press, 1992), 103.

[313]did not permit it: Stacey, 393-394.

[314]tried in one jurisdiction: Coates and Morrison, 110.

[315]."against Canadian women": NA RG 338/NWSC, Box 1.

[316]military personnel stationed there: Stacey, 394.

[317]never builds good relations: As late as 2002, major rioting in Korea protested the trial by a U.S. tribunal of two American soldiers involved in a traffic fatality.

[318]which they did not do: Coates and Morrison, 114.

[319]"U.S. Army Gestapo": Coates and Morrison, 118, quoting NAC RG 36/7, vol. 40, file 28-23, pt. 1.

[320]traditional hunter-gatherer life: Coates and Morrison,77.

[321].saw the black soldiers experience: Coates and Morrison, 72-73.

[322]."the gravel magnet": Cruikshank, Julie, "The Gravel Magnet," in Coates, *The Alaska Highway*, 172-187.

[323]activities in the Northwest: Coates and Morrison, 100 and Cruikshank, 180.

[324].in which their children came to live: Interviews, "The Gravel Magnet" a television program of Northern Native Broadcasting.

[325]mumps and meningitis: Coates and Morrison, 77.

[326]15 out of 150 died: LeCapelain, C.K. (Canadian liaison officer) quoted in Coast and Morrison, 77-78.

[327]normal growth rate: Coates, Kenneth, "The Alaska Highway and the Indians of the Southern Yukon," in Coates, K., *The Alaska Highway*, 158. Data from *Canada, Vital Statistics, 1930-1950*.

[328]increased use of alcohol: Coates and Morrison, 83.

[329]Kluane game preserve: Coates and Morrison, 91.

[330]"rather than an international one": Grant, 71.

[331]"to order Canada around": Grant, 71.

[332]"built by American money": Grant, 78.

[333]head of the Canadian diplomatic office in London: Grant, 101.

[334]visited the area; Grant, 86.

[335]"same powers as a military occupation": Grant, 85.

[336]NAC, King Papers, MG26 J4, 304/3282.

[337]*Idem.*

[338]Toronto, Oxford University Press, 1943.

[339]"will she deserve to": Grant, 113, quoting Beattie, Robert, "Memorandum on Trip to Northwest, 12 April 1943," Department of External Affairs, Historical Records Division, file 52-B(s).

[340]in an Oregon newspaper: Grant, 91-92.

[341]"in payment of war debts": Grant, 125 from WIB Survey No. 14, July 3, 1943 in NAC RG 2/18, vol. 50, file W-34-2-5.

[342]."the best thing for Canada": Diubaldo, 183.

[343]."the North West Staging Route a Polish Corridor": Nordman, 91.

[344]"for the sake of irritation": Trudeau, P.E., *Speech before The Empire Club of Canada, Toronto,* September 29, 1972.

[345]clear declaration of independence: Domestically, Trudeau brought the Canadian Constitution to Canada from having been under the control, albeit formal, of the British Parliament, a controversial move.

[346]"administration of the United States": 37th Parliament, 1set Session, *Hansard* 170, Oral Question Period, April 17, 2002.

[347]"into the United States": Leblanc, Daniel, "Canada Open to Missile-Shield Discussion," *Globe and Mail*, December 10, 2002, A4. The journalist, the U.S. State Department,

and the U.S. Embassy in Ottawa all declined to explain the basis for this agreement, which was not explicitly contained in the exchange of diplomatic notes.

[348]"stuck in the middle": Display at the University of Alaska Museum, Fairbanks.

[349]"tenor of Alaskan life": Naske, Claus-M. and Slotnick, Herman E., *Alaska: A History of the 49th State* (Norman, University of Oklahoma Press, 1994), 131.

[350]"belong to Alaska": CBC News North Report, November 7, 2002.

[351]"black Americans and the federal government": Staples, Brent, "Reliving World War II With a Captain America of a Different Color," *The New York Times*, December 1, 2002. Op. ed.

[352]"Sons of the Middle Border": Originally the phrase was used by Hamlin Garland in his autobiography, but he referred to another region. David McCullough in *Truman* also uses the term to apply to his subject.

[353]wanting to go West: American Soldier Survey, *Post-War Migration Plans of Soldiers*, 9. About one-third of southern white soldiers also planned to move out of the region.

[354]similar educational background: U.S. Army, Research Division, Special Services Branch, Some New Statistics on the Negro Enlisted Man, Report No. 2, February 17, 1942, 7. NA

[355]the path to literacy: Boyd, 11-12.

[356]pay his way to dental school: Joseph Haskins interview, October 1, 2002.

[357]"each others' lives" Interview of James Lancaster, October 15, 2002.

[358]"may be efficiently utilized": MacGregor, 52.

[359]performance of the black rifle platoons: All survey data following is from E.T.O, I and E Division, Research Branch, "Opinions about Negro Infantry Platoons in White Companies of 7 Divisions," July 3, 1945. The survey included 250 respondents, all officers and a sample of platoon sergeants in 24 companies.

[360]suppressed the survey: The attitude of the generals is reported in MacGregor, 54-55.

[361]outstripped the whites': American Soldier Survey, "Soldiers Plans for Government Jobs After The Leave The Army", NA.

[362]only 21 years after the war: Interview of Jesse Balthazar, October 2, 2002.

[363]"something better than this": McCullough, 247.

[364]"a natural born American": McCullough, 248.

[365]"on the basis of segregation": Dalfiume, 151.

[366]the state militia, the National Guard: Dalfiume, 159

[367]backed him up: Dalfiume, 164.

[368]"get into trouble": Dalfiume, 167, quoting the Hearings on Universal Military Training.

[369]"efficiency or morale": MacGregor, 312 includes text of Order.

[370]segregation in the Armed Forces: Dalfiume, 172-173.

[371]frequently do not serve: Butler, Remo, "Why Black Officers Fail," *Parameters*, Autumn 1999, 54-69.

[372]"the supreme triumph of war": Morris, *The Rise of Theodore Roosevelt* (New York, Modern Library, 2001), 594.

[373]"hopes of mankind fail with it": Lodge, Henry Cabot, Sen., Speech in the U.S. Senate, August 12, 1919. First World War.com.

[374]"abandonment of the use of force": Statement on the Atlantic Charter Meeting with Prime Minister Churchill, August 14, 1941, *Public Papers of the Presidents, 1941.*

[375]sovereign sensitivities: F.D. Roosevelt's view might be contrasted with Theodore Roosevelt's. As Assistant Secretary of the Navy, he had hoped publicly for the disappearance of the Spanish and British flags from North America. Senator Marcus Hanna of Ohio had exclaimed: "You're crazy Roosevelt! What's wrong with Canada?" Morris, *The Rise of Theodore Roosevelt*, 624.

[376]"security of the American people": Bush, George W., President, State of the Union Address, February 1, 2003.

[377]"need anybody's permission": Bush, G.W., Press Conference, March 6, 2003.

[378]"remains a sovereign state": Brunt, Stephen, column in *Globe and Mail*, April 1, 2003.

[379]"quite a beating as a result of this": McCarthy, Shawn, "No apologies for ant-U.S. talks from MPs," *Globe and Mail*, April 4, 2003, quoting Paul Tellier, CEO of Bombardier Inc.

[380]indulging its sovereign prerogatives": Interviews with Brian Lee Crowley, an independent observer and former editorial writer for *Globe and Mail* (March 31, 2003), Gerald Doucet, an Eastern conservative and former advisor to Prime Minister Mulroney (April 14, 2003) and James Palmer, a Western liberal and advisor to Paul Martin, candidate for Prime Minister (April 22, 2003

INDEX